THE CIVIL WAR,

PAPA & ME

Family Stories from 1863 to 2012

Catherine Mooney Henson

Contents

Preface

My purpose in writing down these memories that I cherish so dearly is to share them with the people who seem to hunger for more whenever the past is mentioned. I want to share with my many relatives who did not hear my dad tell tales of the past and who could not see the softness he showed in ruling his 13 children. I am the 12th child and I am now 91.

The stories begin with the birth of my dad, James Franklin Marion Jackson Mooney, in 1863 during the Civil War. The stories span over 150 years. These are the tales that captivated us as children. We could not get enough, especially of those told to him by his mother, because it was our only way of knowing her. My own mother had precious memories, too, that we were privileged to hear. Many of the more recent stories are from my own recollections.

I started putting these stories out on Facebook and, as I did, more would come to me. The volume of my writing finally reached a crisis level. I would start out each morning to do daily chores. As I would reach the kitchen door, it was as if a force turned me to the right away from the kitchen; instead, I would find myself at the computer writing another great happening. There I would stay for the next few hours with thoughts just pouring out. My strong desire to preserve these memories for my family – to let them know their ancestors – drove everything else from my mind.

I am thankful to have been able to write this book and for all the things Heavenly Father has allowed me to do. I am thankful for so many, many blessings that he has showered me with. I am thankful for those times when I have been deep into genealogy for someone and then all of a sudden think: I will go ask Mama! – who has been dead for a while. That has more than once sharpened my focus.

Some of the genealogy – which is not a part of my stories – can be found in the appendices to this book. This information is provided by my niece, Judy Martin Underwood, who has done much research on the Mooney family. For that I am grateful and for the many hours she spent editing this book. And credit goes to my talented granddaughter, Cindy Pike, who designed and created the cover. I am indebted to them both.

I feel lots of love for the family that is here and those who have passed on. Among the three of us remaining, there is a closeness that I cannot express. I would like to dedicate this book to my wonderful sisters: Betty Jo Mooney Taylor, who is 89, and Pauline Mooney Henderson, who is 98. They each helped me remember.

James Franklin Marion Jackson Mooney

Franklin was hiding from the enemy. He could hear them, tramp, tramp, over the hollow log that concealed him, frightened, cramped and uncomfortable, waiting for the enemy to leave. After some time had passed and they were gone, he slipped quietly into his home to find something to relieve his hunger and help regain his strength.

Elizabeth, his wife, who was nine months pregnant, was quietly sitting in a kitchen chair, hoping beyond hope that her husband would not be discovered. She greeted him lovingly with all the warmth she felt for him. He hurriedly ate the food she provided, so he could look for a better place to hide, still not confident that he was hidden well enough. Those were distressing hours for Franklin, but he was willing to take the risk to be near his wife when the baby was born.

Elizabeth shared her home with another lady, whose husband was also at war. She had helped Elizabeth through her pregnancy. In the lonely hours, they had each other's company, providing a little cheer. She had shared the tasks of feeding and looking out for Franklin after he came home. Sometimes the women would take biscuits and slip them into his hiding place, always being careful not to cause any disturbance or draw anyone's attention to what they were doing. The Union Army was all around these parts and he knew he would have to return to his regiment, but nothing, he felt, should tear him away from his wife until this baby was born.

Before long, Elizabeth was laboring in pain, with her husband and her friend at her side. And thus my father was born, on May 5, 1863. All was well for now with mother and baby, but hovering over them was this crazy war that was tearing so many families apart.

Franklin stayed in hiding, but close by his wife for the next two weeks, until he felt they would be all right. Then he returned to his post.

It was hard for Elizabeth to see her husband leave. They had not even had a chance to name the baby. She had wanted Franklin to decide what their son would be called.

The hours were lonely for Elizabeth even though she had a baby boy to take care of. Her longing for Franklin was so great – often she would cry herself to sleep.

Technically, Franklin was a deserter; however, this was a common thing during the Civil War. Many men left to see about their families and returned to their regiments. Generally, it was tolerated if not condoned, as long as they returned. Franklin had chosen a name for his son, but he knew he could not leave again and there was no mail or other way to communicate with his wife. Fortunately, one of his fellow soldiers and closest friend, Henry, was able to help. He had told Henry about the situation and what the baby was to be named. Henry had reasons of his own for taking a temporary 'leave.'

Two weeks later, Henry found a means to get away and to deliver Elizabeth a handwritten note from her husband with the cherished name. Like Franklin, Henry had to make his way through enemy territory to deliver the name. Elizabeth, grateful for the letter and for news of Franklin, fed Henry well before sending him on his way, hopeful for his safety. He was able to slip away without notice to take care of his own affairs.

The boy's name was to be James Franklin Marion Jackson Mooney. The James was his own; Franklin after his father; Marion, after Marion the Swamp Fox of Revolutionary War fame; Jackson after Stonewall Jackson.

Two months after returning to the war, Franklin died from exposure, leaving his young wife alone to fend for herself. Sad, depressed and separated from her own family, Elizabeth struggled on

4

with the help of her friends. The war would be over before she was able to reunite with her family. When our President Abraham Lincoln was assassinated on April 15, 1865 by John Wilkes Booth in the Ford Theater, it was 17 days before my dad turned two years old.

My dad's mother was not the only Elizabeth in the Mooney clan to be left widowed by the war. Franklin's mother Elizabeth had been widowed two years earlier. His father was Boaz Mooney.

Boaz

Boaz was born in 1814. Elizabeth was born in 1817. In 1861, at the very beginning of the war, they lived in Baileyton, Cullman County, Alabama. Elizabeth and Boaz Mooney had eight children, Franklin being the second. The first child was a daughter named Marion or Mary Ann. After Franklin came Isabella, Jane Buncombe, George W, Martha, Elizabeth, and Pierce. George W. would fight for the Union side. Pierce was too young to enlist.

Boaz was a blacksmith by trade. He was a good man and a good provider. He was too old to join the fight, but he served the cause in his own way by helping out his neighbors, mostly women and children who were struggling to get by without their menfolk.

Boaz was to be the first death the Mooney family would experience in the war. Boaz did not die gloriously in battle or from disease as so many did. He was murdered by a marauding band of Confederate-leaning vigilantes on the 14th of February, 1861.

Boaz, his daughter Jane and his wife Elizabeth were the only ones at home that day. The younger children were spending time with an aunt. Twelve men on horseback rode up to his house and called his name. The men were armed but not in uniform. Boaz looked at the men on horseback, sensing no good. He asked, "What do you want?" Their words to him were "Come out, old man, we want to talk to you. We hear you been feeding the layouts." The 'layouts' were men allegedly hiding out, refusing to fight for the Confederacy.

He answered forcefully, "I have not seen any of them." He assured them that he had been taking care of only his own people. They ordered him to shut up or they would shoot him. He replied, "Shoot and be damned, you can only beat me out of a few years anyway." These words have been handed down in my family since 1861. They ordered him onto his horse and he obeyed. Later they came back and burned the house. His family would never see him alive again.

It was nine days later that his body was discovered. He had been tied to a tree and shot several times. Bullets had gone through the old beaver hat that he had made himself. There was a note pinned to the tree that said, "The same thing will happen to any man who touches him."

When he was found in the woods, the *men* did not touch him. It was the women who cut him down, wrapped him in an old quilt and dragged him to a wild cherry tree. He was buried there in a shallow grave. Poor Elizabeth and her 17-year old daughter Jane, stunned with grief, horror and despair, had to find a place to live and carry on. The older children had already left home and were on their own.

I have a story that was printed in the "Decatur Daily News" in 1964. It was an interview with James Mooney (a grandson of Boaz and son of Jane) and his wife, Mary Ann Yates Mooney. Many of the details about that day came from this article. The interview was about Mrs. Mooney and the bullet-riddled hat. They remembered her as a sad old lady wearing a black sunbonnet. The story says she went stone blind with grief and brooding.

Elizabeth

So much is NOT known about my grandmother after James was born. She reunited with her family, but when and where is a mystery. Her parents Perry and Martha Widener were in Tennessee in 1870, but she was not with them at that time. So sometime before 1880, she moved with Perry and other Wideners to Mississippi County, Arkansas. The Wideners were very good people, well respected in the community. Papa was close to them but lost contact with his father's people, the Mooney clan.

Elizabeth was lonely and she wanted a home of her own. She became interested in a man she thought could provide that home. Not knowing too much about him, she married him. He was certainly nothing like her Franklin; he turned out to be an unbelievably cruel man who mistreated my father terribly. Papa said that once he whipped him until he wet his pants. Then the terrible man made him lick it up till his tongue bled. My dad said he received much abuse from his cruel stepfather. That marriage was short lived.

One day while her husband was gone, she took her son and slipped away. They walked down to the river and started following a path, but strangely, she seemed not to know where they were going. She started easing out into the water as if in a trance, all the time holding Papa's hand. Papa said as the water began to get deeper, he became frightened and started pulling back. That seemed to bring her back to her senses, and she moved back to the shore and took up the path again. His belief was that she had more than she could handle and wanted to put an end to it. She never married again.

Elizabeth went back to her parents and resumed a more normal life, but when Papa was 12 years old, she died, leaving him an orphan.

Papa

Papa made his own way from then on. He worked for and lived with other people until he was old enough to be his own keeper. He learned many skills and would eventually put them all to use. He was good in most of these things. He became an excellent carpenter. He learned more about farming. He also knew the art of a blacksmith. Among other skills, he could shoe his own horse. He taught himself English, mathematics and other subjects he would have learned in school, had he had a chance to go past the second grade.

Papa had a bit of an entrepreneurial streak. Not only did he have that, but he had integrity and believed in hard work. There was a time when he had a horse-drawn merry-go-round as a business. The last time I was at Knott's Berry Farm in California, it was on display close to the front entrance. I don't know how it got there, but it's gone now. I wish I knew where.

Jennie

As a young man, almost 21, Papa decided to get married. Sarah Jane Peterson was the bride's name and she was 6 years older. They married November 19, 1882. Papa had land that he had acquired through carpentry work, and already had a site for a home. After he and Jennie were married, he built this magnificent home for her. It had 11-foot ceilings and three large bedrooms. It was quite elegant for the times. Papa was happy with his accomplishments and his home.

Being the industrious person that he was, he increased his holdings with animals, outside buildings, fences and other necessary things for a farm home. Papa still had out-of-town work as well and was away from home some. He and Jennie had one child. They named her after Papa's mother Elizabeth. She was called Mary Elizabeth.

Elizabeth seems to have been a very popular name in those years: Elizabeth Mooney, Boaz's wife; Elizabeth Widener Mooney, Franklin's wife, and now Mary Elizabeth, James's daughter.

Mary Elizabeth was the apple of Papa's eye. After having gone so long without a family, he became an enchanted man. He had something to work for and save for. A complete new life had opened up to him and he yearned to be successful.

Papa's happiness was not to last. What happened with Jennie is something of a mystery. He divorced her and there are conflicting family stories about her and about the reasons for the divorce. Whatever the reason, Jennie seemed to be out of his life until something unforeseen happened. All of Papa's animals got out during a storm, while he was gone on a business trip. The animals were scattered over the pasture. The rain had flooded the fields. Jennie took it upon herself to get them all gathered up and out of the flooded area. She saved them, but at a high cost: she became very ill as a result of her lengthy exposure to the elements. She took pneumonia and died. To me, what she did was sure evidence that she still loved my father.

The Panther

On one of the trips away from home, Papa had many miles to travel. He was on foot carrying his bed roll. He was tired and needed to rest, so he pulled off his bed roll and spread it out. He lay down and almost immediately drifted off to sleep. Sometime later he awoke with the realization that he was being covered up with leaves. Knowing the habits of animals, he lay very still, until the animal (a panther, he thought) had him completely covered and he sensed he was alone again. He uncovered himself, then put the leaves back to look as if he was still there. To confirm that he was right, he crawled up into a tree to wait. Not long afterwards, the panther returned with his mate and began to uncover the leaves. After finding no food, the panthers left. James's suspicion had become a reality. He stayed well out of sight till all was quiet again, then resumed his journey.

A Dangerous Encounter

On another of Papa's long trips, he stayed in a hotel, one he had used before. He was returning from his work, and had been paid a large sum of money, which he carried in a suitcase by his side. Before going upstairs to his room, he became hungry and ordered some food. While he was eating, a woman kept trying to make up to him. There were two men lingering around also, and he could tell they were connected some way. Being on his own for so long, he had learned to be cautious; he was already suspicious of her intent. He waited, almost sure what was to come next. She was using all her womanly wiles to gain his full attention.

When he went upstairs to his room, he had an eerie feeling. Soon there was a knock on his door. Before he answered the door, he tucked his gun in his belt. There she stood, with a smile on her face and immediately picked up her act where she had left off. She started into the room sweet-talking him all the while. Papa pulled out his gun and said to her, "If you take one step farther, I will shoot." He steered her toward the door, gun in hand, and there stood the two men. Knowing their intention had been discovered, and not wanting the law after them, they fled the scene in a hurry.

Another Panther

Papa faced danger many times in his travels. Once he was building a house for himself. It was almost finished and he was hoping to be able to stay that night in the house. He boarded up the windows, but didn't get to the doors. Too tired to really care, he threw his bed roll on the floor and lay down to rest. Toward morning, he heard noises outside the house. He knew it had to be animals and that they could come in through the door opening. He took out his gun, watching the front door, hoping he would not have to use it. He knew there were lots of panthers in those parts. After it was quiet for a while, he was able to get a little nap. Next day, bright and early, he made the door and put it up, counting his blessings that no animal had tried to enter. He continued work on his house and made everything secure. The next night he slept with no anxieties, feeling very safe with the door intact. The very next morning, he went outside and discovered panther tracks leading up and down as if the animal had been pacing and had sensed someone was in there.

The Luckett House

Papa was still working and acquiring property, at that time mostly land. He always did well financially. Papa built a lot of houses, many in Dell, the town I grew up in. He was well known for his expert carpentry. Somewhere along the line, a Doctor Luckett moved into the town and was looking for a home for himself and his wife. He was attracted to one particular house that Papa owned, but Papa was sentimental about this house and was hesitant to sell it. This was the house he had built for Jennie. It was a beautiful home, befitting a doctor; reluctantly, he sold it to the good doctor. Papa had built other houses, but this one was special. In the future it was called "the Luckett house."

Laura

Jimmy became restless after a few years. He began to be interested again in the opposite sex. He had Elizabeth to consider as well; she was about seven by then. She needed a mother and he needed a wife. Laura Gardner seemed like a good fit, so he married her. This occurred in July 1889. He was 26 by then. Laura was 27.

This was not the ideal marriage either. Laura was jealous of his daughter and short-tempered with her. Laura was in ill health for most of their marriage. Papa said sometimes he walked several miles to get her medicine. She used a lot of laudanum as was prescribed in those days. He was on alert about protecting his daughter from Laura, who was impatient and too quick with the tongue lashings. One day he started to work, but decided to stand by the door just outside and wait a little while. Very soon he heard Laura deriding his seven year old daughter, telling her to "just leave us alone." He quietly stepped back in and firmly assured her that if there was any leaving to be done, it would be her. Her answer, "Oh, Jimmy, I am just sick."

They struggled the best they could, Papa being concerned about his young daughter, Laura being ill and Elizabeth being unhappy. Laura eventually became completely bedfast, leaving her husband and stepdaughter to take care of her until her death.

Mary Elizabeth

Mary Elizabeth began to grow up and show an interest in boys. She set her sights on a man who kept her in giggles and made her heart flutter. He was a nice, considerably older man – not a boy – named John August Koehler. He was of German descent; his grandparents had migrated to this country years before. He soon started calling on her and they both fell in love. Needless to say, happiness was her lot.

She was 16 when she married John August Koehler; he was 36. They were married July 30, 1899. In all, they had 11 children, three that lived only one year, and one was stillborn. Of the ones who lived, Otto and Merrion came first. Later she had Rachel, Mildred, Raymond, Herman and Thelma. All the Koehler kids loved their grandparents, and they had much respect for their step-grandmother, even though she was close in age to Mary Elizabeth. With his first daughter and her family living close by, Papa was a happy man.

Anderson Ray

I don't know much about Anderson Ray. He was my mother's father, my grandfather. He died sometime before 1900. After a long day of work, as he reached his yard, he told his family that he was going to die. Strangely enough, that is exactly what happened. He staggered into the house and dropped dead of a heart attack. He left behind a widow with six children to raise, two girls and four boys. My mother Josephine was the fourth one down. The older boys were Will, Cap, then Josephine, Anderson, Annie and the last, Pull. He left them financially secure and they were able to continue on with the farming.

Mama

Just in passing, one of Mama's friends said to her the day after Laura had died: "Isn't it bad about Mrs. Mooney's death?" Mama's feisty answer was, "Heck no. You never know, I just might get her old man," not believing that was remotely possible. She did not know him that well. He was older and out of reach. She was just trying to be flip with a cute answer.

Papa was passing the Ray home about two years after his second wife had died. They had a wooden fence around their property to keep the animals out. He was standing by a plum tree as he spotted Josephine watching him. He plucked a plum and threw it at her, giving her the opportunity to give him a big smile. That was his chance to start a conversation, so he came over to the fence. It was clear to see they were interested in each other. Papa thought she was a charmer from the very first time they talked. Mama was agog that this handsome mature man would seek her out. Their courtship was destined from the very beginning.

They had chances to become better acquainted at church socials and town picnics. Not long afterwards, Papa started courting my mom in earnest. They courted on one end of a very long porch. She sat on the porch, kicking her feet and giggling at his every word. Papa was more mature, but he thought she was about the cutest thing he ever saw. All that red hair dangling around her shoulders and that energetic smile she wore.

Courting on the Porch

On the other end of the porch was her mother – my grandmother – Anna, who was entranced with a certain cute young man who had intentions of courting her, therefore spending as much time as possible on her front porch. He was Wallace Perry. It seemed strange for Wallace to be infatuated with a lady twice his age, but his intentions were real. Soon she was entertaining this young man. Wallace Perry was enthralled with the Widow Ray, calling on her often. He was young, but very much in love with Anna. They married in 1900. He was 19 years of age and Grandma was 43. The odds were against them, but they enjoyed years of love and fun and happiness. He was always faithful to her, the only wife he ever had. Even though she was older and died sooner, he never showed interest in marrying again.

Wallace had come courting to Anna's house too often to suit Papa, since Josephine was closer to Wallace in age than to Papa. My dad, having been exposed to many unsettling things in his youth, did not like the thought of Mama having a stepdad so close to her own age. After Anna and Wallace married, Papa still tried to keep Mama at a distance from them, even though the newlywed couple had eyes only for each other. Papa became concerned and decided to change things. Thus he proposed to Josephine: "I do not like the situation here. I want to marry you and finish raising you to suit myself." Mama, already in love with him, was happy to say yes. Even though Papa was older, I truly doubt that he had the upper hand with Mama even then. On July 17, 1904, they were united in marriage. Mama was 16 and Papa was 41.

Papa could not possibly have known what he was getting into. Mom was a vivacious redhead, full of vim and vigor. She started out with a bang. Their first child, Stella, was the beginning of 13 children, myself being number 12. Willie was next, followed by Magaline Miranda (who went by Johnnie), Lloyd, Franklin, Anna, Floyd (who went by Bud), Pauline, Virginia, Vida Ray, Mary Lee, me and Betty Jo.

Mary Elizabeth and Mama

Sister is what we called Mary Elizabeth, at Papa's insistence. Maybe he wanted her to be recognized as one of us. She was very much a part of our lives. She and Mama were the best of friends. Elizabeth was a very religious person and went to church regularly. She was of the Pentecostal faith and Mama belonged to the Methodist church. Mama went a few nights with Sister until Papa put an end to it. He said, "No more, go to your own church." I think they were staying too late at night and maybe enjoying it. Mama did have all her kids in church – the Methodist Church – at an early age. That was a big part of her life.

Mama and Elizabeth were both having babies around the same times. Papa was acquiring more grandchildren right along with his own children. We were very close to the Koehler kids and got along well. They called Mama and Papa Josie and Grandpa. They lived less than half a mile away. Their last child Thelma was born in 1918, the same year as Pauline. Virginia, Pauline and Thelma were very close to each other. When they were little they played together. As they grew up, they shared secrets. They went to the same events. They dated in a group, on picnics, hayrides and similar events. Virginia was truly in love with the guy that Thelma married, but he was crazy about Thelma. I really do not think Virginia ever had a love that strong again.

Maybe Mama and Papa had times of stress, but I think happiness overtook stress. Mama loved Papa as if he were her whole world. In return, Papa thought he had a jewel. Mama's every move was his delight. They had many years of sheer happiness. I saw that love they shared. In the beginning, she called him Mr. Mooney and he called her Wife. Later she addressed him and referred to him as Papa; he still called her Wife.

Anna and Wallace Perry

Grandma and Wallace Perry began to use up the resources left her by her first husband. They bought a new horse and buggy, and were freely going places and enjoying life. After a while, they began to feel financially stressed, and they found it necessary to sell the land. Papa, always conservative with his money, had the means to buy Anna's land. However, he left her 40 acres to live on till her death, and then it would revert to him. Those acres were at the back of Papa's farm.

Anna was expecting her one and only child by Wallace. It had started to snow. The weather became very bad, leaving no way to get in or out. Anna knew her time was near. She knew the midwife could not make it to her, so she began her own preparations for the delivery. She had a young husband inexperienced in these matters, but she would need his help anyway. The pains got stronger and the baby was trying to be born. She asked Wallace to prop her up so she could help the baby into this world. She personally tied the cord, washed the baby and made him ready to see his dad.

After the child, Edgar, was born, they began to settle down and stay at home more. They enjoyed their little family – happiness was theirs. All her other children were grown and had their own families. Edgar grew up alongside Mama's and Papa's first children. When they began to leave home, so did Edgar. He married and had one child named J.C.

From Dell to Ravenden Springs and Back Again

Papa made his fortune and raised his first children on the rich sandy loam of the Mississippi delta. Stella was his first daughter, born October 3, 1905. Willie, the second girl, was born on July 2, 1907. Franklin, their first son, was the first to be born in Ravenden Springs on January 10, 1909.

Papa had heard of a place in the hills with wonderful healing waters – Ravenden Springs, Arkansas. The springs were well known for curative powers and would become a popular resort. Papa bought 160 acres of land and moved all his family there.

Papa had a hand in building the resort. One side of the hill had been encased with a concrete wall to allow the springs to flow freely. Two sets of stairs were built leading down to the springs where people could drink the water. There was a lovely lounging area at the top of the first steps, which Papa built. It included concrete benches where people could sit and relax. It was a beautiful, delightful and profoundly peaceful place. It was especially popular with young people who were courting.

During the ten years they lived in Ravenden Springs, Mom and Pop had another girl named Magaline Miranda, born October 22, 1910. That name was chosen by Mom's mother, but Papa disliked it and started calling her Johnnie. She went by Johnnie the rest of her life. Then along came Lloyd James born February 12, 1912, followed by Anna Cassie born April 23, 1914 and Floyd Jackson born December 5, 1916.

Franklin

Mama and Papa experienced tragedy in Ravenden Springs. As told to me, Lloyd and Franklin both had spent the night with their Uncle Anderson, Mama's brother. They had eaten some tainted watermelon and became sick from it, so very ill that they were afraid both boys would die. Lloyd did recover, but Franklin did not. He died August 3, 1915. Papa and Mama had a few years to recover before they moved back to Dell. Anna was just a baby and Lloyd was only three at the time of Franklin's death. Mama, being the person that she was, never took the time to properly grieve. She put her energies instead into making life bearable for everyone else.

Anna Perry and World War I

Woodrow Wilson was the President during World War One. It lasted from 1914 until 1918. Most people believed him to be an extraordinary president. He wisely led our country through the war. Many people experienced the unrest of their sons being on foreign ground.

This was a hard time for Anna Perry. All of her sons went to war, with the exception of Edgar, who was too young. Her daughters were married by then, so she felt the absence of all her children. Her sons were on the other side of the world. In France! Only boats could take you there! This in itself felt almost impossible to many.

The anxiety of not knowing what was happening to her sons, no way to hear, not knowing if they would come back alive, was almost too much for her. Her greatest fears were relieved in 1918 when the boys started returning. Cap was injured and came home with a steel plate in his head, but he was able to function for years afterward. The other boys were not injured. Anderson said he had been a drummer boy, but when he was faced with all the fighting, he threw down his drum, grabbed a gun and started firing.

Return to Ravenden Springs

August 8, 1918, Pauline was born in Dell, Mississippi County, Arkansas. She was the eighth child down and the last to be born at Dell. She was still a baby when Papa decided to move the family back again to the land he had bought earlier in the beautiful rolling hills of Randolph County, Arkansas. Ravenden Springs was at the foot of the Ozarks. It was truly a peaceful setting with rich green pastures and lots of gorgeous trees. It was the happiest of times for our family. He rented out the land he owned in Mississippi County.

With the move, Papa retired from farming, with the exception of cattle. He did, however, become active in other ways. Besides the cattle, he got involved in politics and was a man about town. We lived in a big two-story house with a porch surrounding it. Life was wonderful in those days. The girls were delighted to be in such a nice atmosphere. All ready to catch a beau.

Of Courting Age

The older girls began coming of age. The guys came calling on their horses or horse-drawn vehicles, sometimes a wagon, sometimes a buggy. The girls were generally not allowed to go *out* on dates; they entertained their young men on the screened-in porch or in the parlor. Occasionally, one or two of the girls would sneak out, but that's another story. Our parents particularly did not approve of the springs for courtship – it was too secluded at the bottom of the stairs. The rules of courting would be relaxed a little as the younger girls came of age.

This was a big time for Stella and Willie. They were of courting age and happily receiving young men. Johnnie was not far behind. Mama seemed to know everything that happened with them almost before the event took place. For example, Willie and Johnnie decided to check out a country dance nearby. They sneaked out without Mama's knowledge, or so they thought. They were just about to have the time of their lives. Willie met Doc for the first time and was duly impressed. Apparently he felt the same. They were happily flirting and getting to know each other, when suddenly this firm, no-nonsense voice boomed from the door, "Willie, Johnnie, I think you better come home." Now Mama's voice could fill the whole room; everyone knew who had been called out. What a bummer, in real trouble so soon after arriving. However, Willie gained from the experience because Doc sought her out and started calling on her, so to her it was worth getting in a bit of trouble.

Willie and Doc

Willie was excited. She was all but leaping in air. It was time for her to receive her young man, who she felt was the love of her life. Doc Wells drove up in a horse and buggy, and soon they were en route to the springs. While they were traveling, the horse passed gas rather loudly, making a big noise. Embarrassed, trying to cover for it, Doc said, "I guess the horse has distemper." Now Willie, not knowing what distemper was, thought he was talking off-color. She therefore demanded to be taken home. She confided in Mama, only to find out what distemper really was. She took some serious teasing over that.

Willie graduated from the eighth grade, which entitled her to teach in those days. She had a strong desire to teach, but to further her education, she would have had to go to another town and board out. Mama and Papa would not have allowed that, so she made plans to remain at home and teach locally where the requirements were not so stringent. However, Doc wanted to get married right away. He promised her if she married him, she could still teach. She married him with that intention. Of course, she quickly became pregnant with her first baby, Maryan Ruth, making a teaching career impossible. Melroy was born next, followed by Thomas Mooney.

Stella and Willie and their families moved to Dell during the Depression, along with the rest of us. Doc and Willie lived on Papa's land in a small cottage. There was a bridge that led over a deep ditch to a road that turned left to go to their house. The road that turned right went to where Stella and Kirb Cook lived. The daughters lived not even a mile apart. Most everyone in the country had shallow pumps for their drinking water. Not deep-well, but shallow pumps that did not always produce good water. Sadly, the water in the deep ditch was bad. Little Thomas Mooney, in his second summer, when he was old enough to drink the terrible water, became sick and died.

Stella and Kirb

Stella and Kirb had three children when they moved to Dell. Kirby James, Laverne and Sybil were well and healthy. But the next three were not so fortunate. Like Willie and Doc, they didn't know about the dangers of polluted water or what you could do about it. Simply boiling their water could have prevented the deaths of their children. Stella and Kirb lost three babies in a row. All died when they turned two and started drinking the water. They were Billy Jack, Grace and one other, whose name I don't know.

It was said in those days, if you could get your baby past the second year, it had a good chance of making it. When I was older and Mama and I were walking over the farm checking out the crops, I decided to get water from the pump. It tasted terrible and smelled bad, reminding us that if they had only known to boil the water, four babies might have grown into adults. After Stella and Willie moved from that area, there were no more young deaths. A very wise choice, since Stella ended up having 12 children in all.

Johnnie and Bryan

Doc needed a haircut. Willie and Johnnie went with him to the barber shop. A cute young barber named Bryan Turner was cutting his hair. Doc introduced Johnnie to him. Oh, he was cute, Johnnie thought. She could not help watching him and flirting a little; and she did get his attention. He was the most popular bachelor in town, and she was sort of in shock when he began calling on her. They courted for a while. And then, in Johnnie's words: "I was just sitting there when suddenly I heard Bryan asking Papa if he could marry me." How could she refuse a proposal that so many girls would have wanted. She was so young and feisty and happy. However, I believe she might have been a little young to settle down.

Johnnie was 15 when she married Bryan. They lived at Dell and her parents were at Ravenden Springs. I feel sure Johnnie loved Bryan very much, but every time someone came by on the way to Ravenden Springs, Johnnie went home. She would stay a few days and Papa would take her back to Dell. It seemed plain that she did not want to be away from the rest of us; but Papa believed in 'once married, till death do us part.' He knew very well where Johnnie belonged. Johnnie and Bryan had two girls named Mary and Louise. Johnnie began to grow up after that.

Life in the Hills

Mama and three of her daughters were expecting at the same time. Mama was in Ravenden Springs and the daughters, Johnnie, Willie and Stella, were in Dell. It was Mama's last baby. Her water broke without the labor. She knew there would be complications if the baby was not born soon. Needing someone to talk to about it, she sent a letter to her girls in Dell sharing her concern. Of course, by the time they had received the letter, Mama had gone to the doctor and Betty Jo had been born.

However, since there were no phones, how could the girls know this? They took one of their husbands' cars and raced home to Mama, leaving three distressed husbands behind. When they got there, mom and baby were fine. They took care of her for a few days before they headed back.

We had lots of good times in the hills. We played in the woods, with big round rocks for a play house. One was a table; it was a big flat rock. The ones just shorter would be the seats. We took our own dishes and played house. I cannot think of a happier time in my life. I must have been about four, but I will never forget the joy that we had in the very green pasture with all the trees. No bugs or flies, just pure happiness, with that warmth from the sun and all those big flat rocks for any purpose that you might imagine.

I was about four when Joe Decker, the town drunk, came to our door. Of course, we never saw drunk people so his strange ways scared all of us kids. We had two Joe Deckers in our town, but this one was not the nice respectable one. He was the nephew, and this day he did nothing to help his reputation. He had been around our house before, trying to find his way home. I think we were warned about him, but he was too drunk to do any harm except to himself. I remember Mama saying to him, "Now go home, Joe Decker, you need to be home, not here." He muttered something about not knowing the way home. He went from one screen door to the next on the wraparound screened porch trying to come in. He was strictly inebriated, though we kids did not know what his problem was. I especially was very scared. Mama went across the street to get Mr. Higginbotham to take Joe Decker home.

A few days later while this was still fresh in our minds, we were downstairs playing in the dining room, having fun, when I just happened to look to the top of the stairs and coming down these stairs was a man with an old black suit on and a walking cane in his hand, with a hat that looked a little big for him, saying in a shaky voice, "I am Joe Decker, I am Joe Decker." He kept repeating himself. And he kept coming down those stairs. I panicked and started running around the very long dining room table trying to escape this horrible creature. I was ahead of him too, but I made the mistake of looking back, still running, and I ran into the table, practically knocking myself out. The next thing I knew, this person – now without the hat – with red hair tumbling down, had me in her arms, rubbing my face tenderly, saying, "Are you all right?" Never in my life have I been so happy to see my mother's face. Of course that ended that game. With all Mama's games and energy, she ensured us a full happy life. Someway, somehow, my mother knew what to do to keep us occupied and out of trouble.

Mama taught us to respect our dad. To this end, when we did something that she disapproved of, she would say, "You do not want me to tell your dad, do you?" Now Papa was as gentle as a lamb, but that was Mama's weapon. Papa, being 25 years older, left most of the disciplining to Mama. No way would we want to hurt our dad. We gained respect for Papa at least partly through Mama's words. The most amazing thing of all, my parents never argued; sometimes they disagreed a little, but Mom had a way about her that tamped down arguments. Sometimes she walked away from a disagreement, but never argued back.

In this wonderful town of Ravenden Springs, Mama was the crème de la crème of society. Papa and Mr. Higginbotham, who lived across the street, were the town's leading citizens. It is no wonder that when we moved away, the girls hated our comedown in society.

24

Mama's Wild Ride

My dad had a real love for cars. He once owned a Saxon, and then he settled into the Dodge line and never left. Mama developed the idea that she would learn to drive one of the new Dodges. We had a car shed at the end of a lane. On one side of the lane was a rock fence and the other side was a pasture with cedar trees. We were in the hills at that time and there was a slight incline. Mama made us sit on the rock fence while Lloyd showed her how to work the gears and the pedals. She managed to get it in gear and started out really great, but as the car gathered speed going down the hill, she forgot where the brake was. She had to decide between the rock fence or the meadow with the cedar trees. She went for the meadow and circled around a few trees, with Lloyd running right behind her, hollering, "Mama, put on the brakes! Put on the brakes!" On the rock fence, out of harm's way, we were also shouting and crying, "Put on the brakes!" It was very exciting – Mama gone wild with the car. Somehow, she got it stopped, but I don't think she ever found the brakes. It was a few cars later before she tried again.

Anna and Clarence

Anna became old enough to date. She was dating a very nice person named Boyd. He really fell for Anna and was so in love with her. Then along came Clarence Grice, at which point Anna fell in love. They were married and made their home in Dell. Clarence was rather outgoing and made most decisions; Anna remained the sweet, quiet and loving person that she had always been. They had two children, Peggy and Barbara, who were adorable to us all. Clarence invariably had a venture going; there was always something new under way. Anna was calm and accepting of whatever Clarence came up with.

Edgar

Anna Perry was getting older. Edgar, her last child, had left home and now had a child of his own. His mother felt so close to this son. She was closer to him than the children born in earlier years, and being Wallace's only child, they spent much time together.

Even though Edgar wanted to be close to home, he needed more money for the needs of his family. When the opportunity came along, he took a job in California. His plan was to be back when he had saved enough.

Time passed. They received a postcard from him saying he had finished a job and would be home before long. The elation his mother felt was extreme. She really wanted to jump for joy. So did his dad. They waited, happily preparing for his return. As more time passed and he had not returned, Anna and Wallace became anxious. There was no way to contact him, nothing to do, only wait and hope.

Anna began to sit on the porch watching for Edgar. Every time she saw someone coming down the road, she thought it might be him. Many more days she sat watching as doubt began to creep into her mind; she began to wonder if possibly something could be wrong. Still not giving up her vigil as the weather got colder, she continued watching from the window. She sat in an old rocking chair, rocking and watching and praying for Edgar.

She pondered on what might have happened. He had written a letter saying he would be home. It was time – it was well past time. He should have been here long ago. Her mournful thoughts went on. *Oh, Edgar, where are you? You were meant to be gone only a little while. You are my last-born child, the only child born to Wallace and me. Your wife and baby need you.*

She finally came to believe that he might be dead, because she knew he would never desert his family. Years passed, but he never returned.

Entertainment

When Lloyd and Bud were about 12 and 13, they decided to go to the springs for a swim. They were enjoying themselves immensely when several troublesome boys decided to torment them. They took Lloyd's clothes and refused to give them back. They knew Lloyd would not come out of the water in the nude. After they had tormented him to tears, Lloyd had all he could take; he whispered to Bud to go get the gun. Bud slipped from the water unnoticed. Without any hesitation, he grabbed his clothes, putting them on as he ran, as fast as his legs would carry him, heading straight for the house.

As he entered the house, he did not slow down for anyone's consent. He rushed into the room where Papa kept the shotgun standing, fully loaded. His clothes were damp as he hurriedly started out of the room with the shotgun over his arm. Mama stopped him and asked where he was going with the gun. He explained that Lloyd had a rabbit treed and he needed the gun right now. He rushed out the door. Mama, being dutifully concerned, went to tell Papa that he should check out the rabbit story. Papa knew the boys would be at the springs. He arrived just in time to hear Bud say, "All right, give him his clothes and leave." The mischievous boys, looking down the barrel of a shotgun, threw his clothes on the ground and headed out in a run.

Bud seemed to be full of ingenuity. He was a solemn boy, rather quiet, but full of ideas. Some bad. In fact, most bad.

Once he built a merry-go-round. He took big wheels from a farm vehicle, put them on a pole and tied a rope so it would act like a merry-go-round. When he had a couple of passengers, he proceeded to make it go around. It made at least half a circle before it came tumbling down, sadly, right on Vida's head. Poor Vida was knocked down by the wheel and had a big gash in her head. Bud knew for sure he was in trouble, but instead of thinking about Vida, he was more interested in covering up his misdeed. His sisters were also trying to keep him out of trouble. They gathered up all the toboggans that were available and put them on Vida's head, so if it bled through one, another would catch the blood. Vida had to be uncomfortable but, faithful to her brother, she endured.

It was not long till supper, and we all gathered at the table. After the prayer was said, Mama reprimanded Vida, "You know you don't wear a cap to the table, so take it off." Vida took off the first toboggan, then the next. It was the third before the blood began to show. Of course Mama was aghast at her condition, and immediately tried to doctor it. I really do not think brother Bud got into too much trouble, as they were too busy taking care of Vida. I am sure they used soot from the wood stove to pack the cut to keep it from bleeding too freely.

Our Own Kind of Play

We had a different way to play than today's children. We made our own toys. We knew how to take a long pole and nail tin cans on it to make tom walkers. We could walk high in the air with those tom walkers. We knew how to make our own bats and used twine to construct a ball. We had lumber and hammers and plenty of nails. Baling wire was always available. The real fun came from these everyday things.

Most of our play time was outside and resulted in many bruises. We were all very good at climbing trees, and I could go as high as anyone. I think I might have been a bit of a daredevil. You have heard that expression 'up a tree' – well, that is where we usually were in those days.

Mama played with us a lot. We had water fights. We played hide and seek and so many other games. We cut paper dolls and clothes to match out of the Sears & Roebuck catalog. Papa was older and slower, but Mama was full of energy and ideas that kept us busy. She was also full of wisdom. She knew how to keep our language clean and our thoughts in the right direction. No cards allowed at our house. No danger of ever having gambling thoughts. I was grown before I played a game of Pitch. No speaking evil. Absolutely no slang at all.

Once Vida and Mary Lee were playing a game and Mary Lee made a mistake; she said, "Well, I'll be dog." Vida started yelling for Mama to repeat what she had said. Mary Lee's reply was "I did not, I said I'll be pig." Of course Mama saw humor in that. This lesson stayed with me until I was almost a teenager in school at Dell. I occasionally would hear my friends using the Lord's name in vain. One day when I was alone, walking on the sidewalk at school, I decided I would try using those words in my expressions. The experiment lasted one day, because every time I spoke the Lord's name in vain, it was as if I had been pricked with a knife. That was the end of my using God's name in such a manner.

Church-going

Mama was of the Methodist faith. We all went to church; in the early years so did Papa, but as time went on, he did not go as much. We did not misbehave in church either. We were always on the front row. I sometimes wondered why the third row would not be as good, but it was always the front row. If you misbehaved a little, Mama had this special pinch she used and, if the behavior was not corrected, that pinch had a twist to it. She did keep us all in check.

During a revival, it was nothing for Mama to have five preachers over for a Sunday dinner. We had a very long table, but not long enough for everybody, so the adults ate first, then the children. I got so hungry at times waiting on the adults to leisurely eat and have a conversation. When I became a mom, my kids ate first if there was not enough room at the kitchen table. No messing around waiting on adults.

Aunt Annie

One of our most exciting pastimes was to spend the night with Aunt Annie. She always had some spooky tales. She had all kind of stories of ghosts and goblins and was sure that the devil was after Charlie, her husband. He probably was too. Charlie always seemed to be gone. Aunt Annie and Charlie Marrs had three girls. Their names were Dovey, Thelma and Eula Bea. They were our friends.

I do not know why Aunt Annie had such a vivid imagination. I wonder if she did without so much that her daydreams took over, or if she just liked to tell stories that filled our imaginations. I think all her fun was in the kids. Once when we were spending the night, she came up with this creation. She told us about a trunk upstairs that was haunted. The devil had chased Charlie though the upstairs window. Aunt Annie had heard his chains and the trunk had become haunted through this encounter. If you sat on this trunk, it would start moving. It would creep out away from the wall. I absolutely could not let this opportunity pass. We went upstairs to play and I decided to sit on the trunk to see what would happen. Sure enough, I leaned back against the wall and the trunk started moving away from the wall. Now if you are just a kid with a strong imagination, you could believe she was right. However, sometimes you had to push a little harder against the wall to get it to magically move.

We did other things too. We did a lot of crawdad fishing. With just a little bit of salt pork on the string, those crawdads would really hang on. Aunt Annie would clean them and fry the tails – which I would never eat.

One of our favorite things was to make molasses candy. She would help us get it going. When it got to the string time, we all took candy and started stringing it until it was just right to cut. Aunt Annie had wood floors. We were always barefoot and if we dropped any candy, we would step in that hot taffy. We also took material and thread to her house, and we would cut out the material and make rag dolls. Sometimes we would take good material that we were not supposed to have, and she would tell Mama. Mama had so much more then Aunt Annie that I am sure she made a point of sending more of everything than necessary, especially sugar and food. Mama might have furnished groceries, but Aunt Annie furnished fun and excitement.

One night, she told us a story of a mysterious sister that I knew nothing about. From her lips came this story.

The Mysterious Mary

It was Christmas time and everyone was so excited. They were having special desserts and eggnog. The children ate heartily. Not very long afterward, the kids begin to get sick – very sick – making everyone worried. There were several children in the group, so the adults began checking the kids, one by one, to be sure they were all right. One of the relatives saw Mary over in the corner, too still and not making any noise at all. She hollered for the mother. Mary was not breathing. Alarm set in and they started working with her, trying to get her to respond. She was lifeless and just lay there. They had all begun to believe she was dead. There was no response at all. Her mother pulled her into her arms and began to cry and call her name. "Mary, Mary," she moaned, "please talk to me." After a few minutes, Mary came alive, her voice filled with excitement, "Oh, Pa, don't ever let the boys be preachers – I saw what happens to them. I came back for a reason, but I will only be here six more months." Now Aunt Annie told us other things that Mary said, but I was small and don't remember it all. But I remember those particular words because they did not sound right. Surely, she could not mean preachers, men of God who were trying to do good. I decided she had to mean only people more interested in money than in Heavenly Father's words.

What really puzzled me was that Mama did not tell us she had a deceased sister named Mary. Was Mom just too busy to mention her? Also, knowing Aunt Annie, I was not sure if she was even real. Whatever the case, it was a mystery that needed solving. I could hardly wait to get home to ask Mama about Mary. When we got home, I followed Mama out to feed the animals and asked, "Mama, did you have a sister named Mary?" She said yes. "Did she die and come back to life?" Mama answered, "Something like that." I asked, "Did she die again in six months." "About that," she said. I wanted to know about what Mary said. Mama just kind of dismissed it. If it was not explainable, Mama did not mess with it anyway. Aunt Annie told other things that Mary said. Someone asked her about a person that had passed on and she said, "Do not ask about them." I believe that Mama, being younger than Mary, either did not understand it or did not remember it.

I had to know about the mysterious Mary, so later on I started digging. What year were you born? I know you did exist. When did you die? I know you were a sister to Josephine and Annie. I know you had four brothers, namely, Will, Cap, Anderson and Judge Pull. I know you were the daughter of Anna Eddings Ray and Anderson Ray. Why is there no record of you anywhere that I can find? Were your records destroyed in fire, flood or some other disaster? I suspect you were born between Will and Mama, which would have been about 1885. I have not thought of you in years, until this week – you hit me like a ton of bricks. You were a person, you had a story, you were alive and active. Had it not been for Aunt Annie, I would not even know about you. Neither would I have known that you had a half-brother Edgar that mysteriously disappeared.

Willie and Doc in Albuquerque

Willie and Doc now had Maryan Ruth and Melroy. They moved to Albuquerque because Willie was in poor health and needed a drier climate. They settled in, Doc found work, and they seemed to like it there. They had another baby boy named Billy Delbert. Mama missed them terribly but she was busy with her own children. The only contact Mama had with them was through the mail, but we stayed close through those letters. They were there for several years.

The Great Depression

Papa had some differences of opinion with the church. One of these happened in 1929, when Herbert Hoover was running for President. Papa liked his opponent, Al Smith. Feelings ran high. Papa felt that Hoover should not become President of our country. He took an active interest in this particular election. When Al Smith did not win, it was too much for my dad. He blamed the church for putting Hoover in. Al Smith was Catholic… and we lived in the Bible Belt.

After the election, when Sunday came, Mama got the kids ready for church. Papa did not go. He refused to send his money to the church. Mama wisely did not argue. She took us all on to church and we enjoyed the Sunday atmosphere, not suspecting anything was amiss. When the next Sunday arrived, we were surprised when she told us we weren't going to church today and we could go to the woods to play. Knowing it was unusual was not enough to keep us from going off to play and have fun.

Papa came into the house and said to Mama, "Wife, just why are you and the kids not in church today?" It was an easy reply for Mama, "Well, Papa, if the church is not good enough to support, it is certainly not good enough for our kids." Next Sunday, Papa brought his money and we all went to church. I feel sure Mama had the preacher over for dinner also.

As it turned out, Papa was right about Herbert Hoover. It did not take too long for the Great Depression to hit. Our world came crashing down. He lost big, like lots of others. He lost a fortune when the banks crashed. Instead of jumping out a window, though, as some others had, he found another way to survive.

Around 1930, Papa decided to sell his land in Randolph County and made plans to move back to Dell, where his other land was. His retirement had come to an end. He sold to the people that had a mercantile store. They did not have all the money up front, but he traded it out until it was paid in full. All of this was fine, because Mama liked to sew for all of us and received material by the bolts from the mercantile store. In each shipment, she would get as many as five big bolts of different patterned materials.

Not as noteworthy, but I recall that it was about this time that peanut butter was invented. The older girls had sampled it in other places and wanted Mama to order some. Anna was raving about it and made it sound like dessert. Mama was apprehensive about ordering food she had no experience with, but when the five-gallon bucket of peanut butter arrived, she grabbed a big spoon and stuffed some into her mouth. Immediately, she started gagging and choking. It was not quite what Mama expected, and it did not function well as a dessert. I'm sure it was not as refined and pliable then as it is now.

Meanwhile, Papa got everything set up for the move to Dell that no one wanted. It felt like a real sacrifice to all the family. We were leaving a beautiful, carefree life, full of leisure, relaxation and friends. We would miss our life in society, as opposed to being an ordinary farm family, with lots of hard work, and without the social distinctions. From carefree happiness to drudgery, it seemed at the time.

Return to Dell

All of this changed Mama. She left off her hat and gloves and her finery for cows to be milked, cotton to be picked, pigs to be slaughtered, chickens to be fed. However, she did not complain; she just went to work. Mama did not really have to go to the fields to work, but I suspect it was a relief to her just to get away from so much housework and so many kids. Mama also took us to the field to work.

This new lifestyle was a shock to the system and we hated it. Lloyd and Bud, Pauline and Virginia were the four oldest left at home; also Vida, Mary Lee, me and Betty. We had moved from a big fancy house to a smaller one without nearly enough room. I remember three big beds in a room – although it was a big room. There were no closets at all.

Papa started adding on. He added two big rooms to the front of the house. One was a living room and the other was a bedroom. He also added a kitchen and a new ice box. Every day the ice man delivered 100 pounds of ice.

In the hills, we had a deep well with wonderful water. Now we had a shallow pump with water not as pure; therefore, we hauled our drinking water from the Indian mounds (more later on that) where there was good water.

The Rain Barrel

Have you ever had the opportunity to wash your hair in rainwater? The water that flows from the clouds is so pure. It leaves your hair so soft and clean without the tangles you get from hard water, thus no need for conditioner. This is why we had a rain barrel.

One of the times Mama was working outside in the field, happy to be in the fresh air, when out of the clear blue she remembered the rain barrel sitting at the edge of the porch. Then she imagined her smallest child – that would be Betty – going up to the barrel, looking in and falling over into it. In horror, she went as fast as her legs could carry her to the rain barrel, fearing the worst. Relief and tears followed her exhaustion. Little Betty was safe, but that rain barrel never got put there again.

"Bring them to me"

Willie. We got the news that Willie had had a baby boy. His name was Malcolm Keith (later on we would call him Mike). We were all overjoyed for the Wells family, but that lasted only a few days. I was about seven years old when that disaster hit us. Mama got a telegram that our sister Willie had died, 11 days after childbirth. During that time that Willie was so desperately ill, Mama had wanted to go to her. Papa had said then, "We don't have much money; we can spend it on a trip or we can send the money to help take care of Willie." Mama decided to send the money.

The telegram was terrible news for us all. Mama became hysterical. She didn't feel she could go. Not only was it more than they could afford, but traveling to Albuquerque was such a long hard trip, and Mama had so many kids depending on her. She felt strapped to home. The decision was really already made, but with Willie's family so far away, she was desperate. I so well remember the distress she was in. She waved her arms up and down, she bent over to the floor, she cried with such agony – just completely out of control. There was no way for her to go to Willie's funeral. Poor Mama grieved with force.

Doc had someone keeping the children for a while. Then he put them in a Catholic orphanage for a few months, at which time he was told he had to take them back or they would be adopted out. The orphanage had separated the boys from Maryan Ruth. This was very hard on the little kids. Doc had a big decision to make. Four children and one a baby – what to do? He did the only thing he knew to do: call their grandma. This propelled Mama into action. She just forgot she had raised 13 of her own. Her words were, "Bring them to me."

The Only Solution. Lloyd met Doc and the children at the train station in Blytheville. Doc was bewildered; he did not know what to do. They arrived home in the car with this little baby and three more. The oldest, Maryan Ruth, was seven years old. She was my age. We watched as these sweet kids got out of the car – so well-kept, so well-mannered they were. Willie had spent much time teaching her children many things. She had always wanted to be a teacher; she must have been putting that to use. It did not take them long to fall in with our way of life.

At that time, Papa was 69 and had not planned on increasing his family. Betty had been born when he was 65. This is when Mama took over.

Mama, always thinking she could change the world, had told Doc to bring them to her. Doc had real plans of staying there and working on the farm, and he did, for a while. I can see how being there would have affected him; I am sure he lost complete control of his children. They were Mama's by then just like the rest of us, Mike especially. He was everyone's baby. Mike, apparently, had had absolutely no loving attention and he was sick and so frail. At first, we carried him on a pillow; he was no longer lacking in love and care. It wasn't long until he started responding to us.

We all loved him and we all took care of him. Being only six weeks old when he got there, Mom was his whole life and the person he loved most in this world. By then his dad was somewhere else. We loved those kids like they were our brothers and sister. Maryan Ruth and I hung out together from the first. She was always so cute in anything she wore. I was tall and gangly – and aware of it.

Maryan Ruth and Melroy called Mama 'Grandma,' but to the little ones, she was 'Mama;' and Papa was 'Papa' to everyone.

Billy was such a serious boy. In a few years, he made contact with his dad, and when he became old enough, he went to work with Doc at the gin. He really never replaced his love for his dad. He and Doc had a special relationship. Now Mike was another story; Mama was his very all.

We were a big family. We certainly did not need many outside friends. With a group that large, we usually did things in pairs. Pauline and Virginia, Vida and Mary Lee, me and Maryan Ruth. Betty teamed up with Willie's boys. We truly did have fun growing up.

Shirley Temple

We – about five of us – wanted to go to a Shirley Temple movie. It was almost a must that we see that movie. We asked Mama to please let us go. I think we got a little insistent with Mama. She told us all to go sit on the couch in the living room until she got ready for the movie. We went obediently to the living room. We were already dressed to go, so sure of ourselves we were. We waited and waited and began to get impatient. When finally, finally, out came Mom. Her hair was in tight

38

little curls standing out from her head. Her dress was short and pulled up to look like a pleated shirt. Her face had lipstick spots all over it. She came in the room with her hands holding out the edge of the skirt, her feet shuffling like she was trying to tap dance. Then she started singing 'The Good Ship Lollipop.' We all just sat there in disbelief, not knowing whether to cry or laugh. I really think we cried then, but we have laughed ever since. Mama must have had shock absorbers to have raised that many kids and keep such a good sense of humor.

Mary Lee

Dating. Mary Lee went on her first date. When she got home, Vida asked her, "How did it go?" Mary Lee said it was good. Vida asked, "Did you like him?" Mary Lee replied that she did. Vida asked, "Did he ask you out again?" Mary Lee: "Yes." Vida: "Well, what did you tell him?" Mary Lee: "I said No." Then Vida said, "What did you say that for?" Mary Lee's reply, "Well, I didn't want him to think I liked him." At that point, Vida decided that Mary Lee needed lessons in dating. She told Mary Lee that she had a date with Harry that evening; they would sit in the swing under the tree, and Mary Lee could learn how to talk to a boy on a date. Mary Lee, who was an expert at climbing trees, was told, "Just sit up there and listen."

It was time for Harry, and Mary Lee was on her perch in the tree. Vida Ray brought Harry around to sit in the swing. He was unaware that he was being observed during this date. I guess Vida said the right things to get the right answers, but Mary Lee got bored. She climbed down from the tree and said to Vida, "I have heard enough," in her sober way, and away she went. Poor Vida was left to explain to Harry that he was the unwilling participant of this scheme. Fortunately for Vida, Harry liked her well enough that he forgave her, and they went on with their date.

Mary Lee's next date was with Cecil Mills. He lived with his grandmother who had been raising him. There were not too many things to do in our little town, so they decided to go roller skating. The only pavement around at that time was the school sidewalks. They soon became bored with such a small area and decided to go to the highway where there was plenty of room to skate. Fortunately, traffic was not too bad in those times. The real drawback was that it was evening. Vida and her date, who were with them, decided to sit on the railroad tracks and just watch and enjoy themselves privately. Mary Lee and Cecil were skating along fine and Mary Lee began to complain of some uneven spots in the pavement. Cecil suggested they change sides. They had barely done so when the lights from an oncoming car, on the opposite side of the road, blinded them so they could not see the lights from a car coming up behind them. The lights also blinded the oncoming car. They were hit from behind. Cecil was killed immediately and Mary Lee was knocked off the highway with a broken leg and other injuries. She was taken to the hospital and Cecil to the morgue. No phones, of course, so it took a while for everyone to get notified. Vida and her date were in shock.

Cecil's grandmother wanted to spend time with Mary Lee because she was the last person to see him alive. Mary Lee did not know quite how to handle that. She never told her how they had just switched sides; otherwise, it would have been her. Mary Lee got well, but never quite got over the shock of Cecil. There were no kids skating on the highway after that.

Mary Lee was especially enamored with one fellow she was dating. One night she got home by the twelve o'clock deadline but was so in love and too wide awake. She came in to me and said, "Get up and let's bake a cake." Seeing how excited she was and realizing her need for company, I crawled out of bed. Then she said, "You bake it and I will ice it." So I made myself wake up, pulled out what was needed, made the cake and put it in the oven to bake. All the time she was dancing around dreaming of her date.

The cake was done and I told her it was ready to ice. Her reply was, "Oh, it is such a bright moonlit night, let's go play tennis." So, since it was a very bright night and we did have a tennis court, I drug my sleep-deprived body out to the court and we played a few games. By this time, it was getting to be daylight and Mary Lee was winding down. She turned to me and boldly said, "I'm getting tired. I need to go to bed. You ice it." I must have been a little dumb in those days because I actually did ice the cake.

Full of Ideas. One time we took our car to town. It was always a new car, but we had no money. All our needs were met, but with that many kids, we surely did not get an allowance. This particular time, we went farther than we were supposed to and ran out of gas. If we were nearer home, we could get gas and just say "charge it." What a predicament. Vida, Mary Lee and I got in a huddle about what to do. There was no way to call home; nobody had home phones. This was indeed a challenge. Mary Lee was the one always full of ideas: "We will call for road service and ask them to bring us gas. After they get the gas in, they can't take it back out. At that point, we will tell them we don't have any money and that we will bring the money back tomorrow when it's light."

We had to walk back three miles to a roadhouse to make the call. That was terrifying in itself. Sure enough, the service truck came, the guy put in the gas, and it was time for Mary Lee's spiel. It did not go over well. The guy had delivered five miles out of town and was disgruntled. Finally, Mary Lee said, "We can leave you our new tire and wheel from the trunk." That was worth more than the gas, so he agreed.

When Papa found out next day, he was a little disgruntled himself. He got in the car, went up to pay the bill and got the wheel back. I often wonder how they stood all that we put them through.

A Flair for Writing. Our English literature teacher said she had taught six Mooney girls and all could write. Mary Lee, however, wrote more than her share in class. Her friends would ask her to write their stories and themes for them. She always wrote Vida's. Vida was reading one of those stories out loud to the class. It was an interesting story that Vida had not bothered to read beforehand. In the middle of the story, from out of nowhere she read, "Elsie was a cow," which pertained to nothing. Mrs. Mullins, our teacher, said, "Vida, who wrote that story for you? Did Mary Lee?" Another time she wrote an assigned paper for several friends; the only thing is, she wrote the same story for each person. She loved playing a trick on anyone she could. Mary Lee was a little more gifted in writing ability, but also full of the devil.

Stella's Kids

Stella lived in Paragould. Sometimes she came for a visit, bringing her children with her. Stella had nine surviving children; three had passed away. Mama and Stella were very close to each other, but that many kids made their visits very difficult. Sometimes when we started to bed, the bed would already be full. I think maybe we weren't very welcoming as a result. Stella realized that, so she spaced her visits and left some of her kids at home with their dad.

Mama and Stella were together one day and decided to go over to town. They and their many kids were in the store, when suddenly Stella said, "Who has the baby?" No one had the baby. She had depended on older kids to carry the baby, but no one picked her up. Panic struck. Everyone loved the baby Janet. They could not get home fast enough and rushed in expecting the worst. There was a stampede to the bedroom…where little Janet lay peacefully sleeping. That was the last time any of us got left off. Stella left in a few days and we got our beds back.

The Indian Mounds

On our land there were two hills side by side. One was a graveyard for the community. It was known as the Mooney cemetery. Nieces and nephews and many more kin were buried there. The other mound had at one time been an Indian burial ground. When playing on that hill, we found lots of Indian relics. We didn't know they would be of value later, and we did not save them. The graveyard was a mound filled with trees that cut off all the air around it. That is where the younger kids, including me, went to use our imagination and scare ourselves half to death.

When there was a death was in the community, the family would ask permission to bury their deceased there. Papa finally had to stop people from using the cemetery because it began to take up the farm land. Though not before I had relatives buried there.

The graveyard was one of our big adventures. There was no one to run you out, no one to disturb you but yourself. We would head to the graveyard with the full expectation of reading the epitaphs and seeing who was buried there. We would always think we could get to the tombstones at the top of the hill, but we never made it that far. By the time we got to the graveyard, we had already spooked ourselves out and didn't stay long. I still don't know who is on top of the hill.

Luxuries

Books and a Lamp to Read By. We had outdoor toilets, equipped with a Sears and Roebuck catalog for toilet paper. I personally never liked to use the page with a handsome man in a suit. We had no electricity at that time; however, we had a wonderful Aladdin lamp that put out bright light for reading and studying. Not everyone could afford that kind of light. We had a long table that we used for homework. We gathered around that table with the bright lamp and studied for hours.

When we did not have homework, someone – usually Virginia – would read a story from the English literature book. We all reveled in a good scary story, like *The Fall of the House of Usher*, or maybe *The Cask of Amontillado* or something else by Edgar Allen Poe. We did know our English literature. We had a set of encyclopedias that Papa had purchased from a traveling salesman. We also had a set of classic books that we read from. Papa really believed we would all be lawyers, doctors or congressmen. He was into education, so he furnished all we needed for a better education. However, that does not mean that our minds worked the same way. Most of us believed in fun first, but we got good schooling along with our fun.

Story & Clark. He purchased a Story & Clark piano for the older kids. It was a self-player and could be converted over to regular playing. It was important to the kids born later as well. I'll always remember that wonderful piano. Papa paid $700 for it; at the time, that amount would have bought a farm. It always sat in the living room for anyone who wanted to play. It was a familiar sound as I grew up.

First Radio. We had the first radio in our area. It was about three feet tall and sat in a corner of the living room. It was a very exciting thing to have. A lot of the neighbors came at night to listen to it. We would listen to a nightly story. Sometimes it would get so exciting and scary, as you listened to a squeaky door opening, or a person walking into a room that was not supposed to be there. It did involve the imagination. I suppose we never lacked for excitement. Papa surely furnished us with the latest things.

44

Fur Coats. You never knew when Papa would have a wild impulse. Once Pauline, Virginia and Vida Ray came in from the cotton patch. Much to their surprise, Papa had purchased each of them a fur coat from a traveling salesman. Wow, such luxury they were not expecting. Real fur too. That was just about the end of their field days, so they had more opportunities to sport their new coats.

The Electric Fence

We had an electric fence for the animals. It just so happened that I knew a lot about electricity, and I knew how to handle the electric fence. I also knew how to play tricks. One of my tricks was aimed at Mary Lee. As one of her chores, she had chosen to pump water for the horses every afternoon. In her mind, it beat washing dishes. This certain afternoon I was all ready for her. I took a big roll of tangled-up baling wire, connected it to the electric fence and put it in the path to the horse trough. It was in her direct path, no way of getting around it. I had big hopes of giving her the shock of her life. I hid, waiting for her, until it was time for the horses to be watered. I kind of lost track of time, though, and got interested in something else. All of a sudden, I heard a Comanche-like yell and tromping of feet; it sounded like the whole tribe was having a war dance. At that point I became frightened. I realized it was Mama hung up in the tangled wire, flapping her arms and yelling. Next I really became frightened, because I knew I was in for it. Fortunately, I had sense enough to unhook the wire to the electric fence and help her get untangled. I think she was so relieved to be saved that I did not even get a whipping.

College of the Ozarks

One day after Pauline and Virginia had finished their last year of high school, they got the surprise of their lives when Papa informed them he had enrolled them in college. In those days, colleges had representatives that called on parents with eligible college enrollees. He had them enrolled in the College of the Ozarks, in Clarksville, Arkansas. It seemed far away but it was close enough. Papa had them paid for and ready to start in a few weeks. They were so excited and could hardly wait. It would be their first time away from home. They could make new friends and have a great time.

Boyfriends

It was summer and college was out. Pauline had been dating the student body president, the most popular guy at school. His name was Al Lopez. He wanted to visit her. I remember that visit so well. We did not know Papa had a prejudiced bone in his body until that summer when Al arrived. Pauline should have informed him that he was from old Mexico and that his family still lived there. If his family had not been pretty well off, he would not have been in school in the United States. Mexico back then was a world away. Papa did not pout in front of Al, but we could feel the tension. He just stayed away from them. Now this was not at all like Papa. Maybe he thought he might lose Pauline to another country. Al never got invited back because Bob Henderson had a fit. Anyway, there had never been any danger of another guy taking Bob's place.

Virginia also had a special friend that she was so in love with. His name was Bill Faucet. He was not in college, but he lived in Clarksville. He did get to visit. Her whole life was caught up with him for a while. Then she kind of lost track of Bill and started dating Carl Martin. Within a year, she and Carl were engaged. In spite of that, Bill decided he wanted to come see her and he did. They parted company for good at that time, since she was engaged to Carl.

Life was not easy for Virginia. After a few years, Carl had become an alcoholic and eventually died from that. Strangely enough, Bill became an alcoholic too. So either choice for Virginia would have

46

ended the same way. She did have a wonderful daughter, Judy, who went through a lot of unhappiness until she finished school and went on her own. Happiness is not always there at first. However, she did gain it with her marriage and her twin girls, Jennie and Rosie.

Pauline and Virginia went two years to school. I think Papa thought they were majoring in fun, because he did not send them back for the third year.

A Horse

I remember when Bud and Lloyd and Papa were working the horses out, and Papa's finger got hung up in the reins. The horse whirled around hard and took part of Papa's finger with it. Papa came to the house to get doctored. None of us could stand to see anything go wrong with Papa. Bud went inside to get the gun; he was going to shoot the horse for hurting Papa. Of course, Mama settled him down – along with the rest of us – and *then* Papa got doctored. In those days, you rarely went to the doctor. If needed, the doctor came to you.

Growing Up on a Farm

Home Remedies. I can easily say I liked everything about my life growing up, with the few exceptions of sorrow. I even enjoyed getting chicken pox; you could get people to run from you. Some things were not so fun, though. For example, I had seen people cutting wood, so one day I raised the axe as high over my shoulder as I could. When I started down with the axe, I didn't have the strength to make it go into the log like I planned, but it did make it to my knee and cut it right to the bone. They packed the wide-open gash with good old soot from the stove to stop the bleeding and help it heal. I am sure there was no hospital close. It did heal with no trouble, but even now I have a big scar on my knee.

I also discovered cold water would heal a bad burn, when Mama got a washing machine. It had a gasoline motor. It was so wonderful. You did not have to use the scrub board. I enjoyed hearing the swish swash as it washed the clothes. It had a long exhaust to take the fumes away. Barefoot as I always was, I stepped on that hot exhaust and burned my foot really bad. I cried, limped around, and tried a few remedies but nothing worked until I put my foot in a pan of cold water. Wow, what relief! I could not stand to have it out until almost bed time. Many years later, I heard that something cold helped a burn. I could have told the medical profession that. I did not even have a scar.

Self-Sufficiency. As Papa was raising his family, he continued to buy land. He worked at farming, at carpentry, at blacksmithing, and was generally self-sufficient. We had a huge garden. We raised our own vegetables and canned them. We raised animals and the corn and hay needed to feed them. We even shucked our own corn and took it to the mill to grind our corn meal. We didn't need to buy much, but it was so exciting when Papa would bring in a ten-pound stick of bologna or a ten-pound box of cheese. He traded at a wholesale house, as he kept a commissary for the people that worked the land. They settled up with him in the fall of the year. In those days, you did not just run to the grocery store. It was either on hand or you did without. Many times Papa had his own tobacco hanging. Most times he did not smoke, but it was there if he chose to.

Hog killing time – to me – seemed wonderful. We never had less than three hogs to butcher and we had lots of help from neighbors. The neighbor kids came and played while their parents worked. Everyone took home fresh meat. It took forever to grind up all that tenderloin for sausage patties. We all had a hand in that. Next day Mama would take the big black kettles and build a fire around them and make cracklings. She cooked the pork all day until the meat was brown and could be made intro cracklings. I still love crackling cornbread. We cured our meat and it was put in the smoke house to be available until the next spring. We always had delicious hams and plenty of salt meat. Everything else we needed was in the pantry.

Financial Security. Mama had a source for her personal money. She separated the cream from the milk. She had a big cream separator that held five gallons of milk. It had three spouts, one for skimmed milk, one for the whey and one for the cream. We all had a hand in turning the separator – there was nothing electric in those days. I will say that all of these things kept us physically strong.

After the separation process, she put the cream in a five-gallon can and took it to the train station. It was shipped to Jonesboro, where it was picked up the same day to be processed. She received a check monthly for this enterprise.

As Papa became more secure financially, material things were more plentiful. Every year he bought a new Dodge. Even though he did not drive very much, he had plenty of drivers at his disposal. We always had lots of salesmen coming around when it was time to trade for a new model – but always a Dodge and always black.

Mama was independent and did not like to ask Papa for money. I can understand that feeling. Mama and Papa occasionally had a difference of opinion about money. Once when Mama was going to Blytheville with Virginia and Pauline, in Papa's new car, of course, Mama told Papa she needed a little money. He took out his billfold and pitched it to her. She just picked it up and threw it back to him. Papa always had money in his billfold, usually a lot of it.

A New Look for the Living Room

When Pauline and Virginia began dating, they asked Mama if we could buy a new living room set if they earned the money for it. Not only did Mama OK it, she went to the field and worked with the girls until they earned enough money to buy it. They went to the furniture store and picked it out, to be delivered later. It was delivered and set up and made the living room look very nice. They were super happy with it. Everyone was but Papa. He thought they were being too frivolous, so he went off to pout. He went out with his walking cane and opened the door to his new black Dodge. He sat down, stirring the sand with his cane, with a downcast look on his face. Mama came out and said to Papa, "Now Papa, those girls earned their own money to buy the furniture. They worked hard for it. So you do not need to be upset." Papa's answer was, "Wife, what is this world coming to? Are we finally going to have to separate?" Mama replied, "Well, I don't know, Papa. Where would you go?" Papa stirred the ground again with his cane and sat there a while. By the time he came in, he knew he had lost. So he got in a better frame of mind and accepted the new living room furniture.

The Seasons

In the summertime, we had no fans; there was no way to stay cool. When the weather got sultry hot, we would make pallets and sleep on the screened-in front porch. Thank goodness for that screened-in porch. Sometimes there would be six or seven pallets. In the middle of the night when a breeze would come up, it would feel so good. What sweet relief. Of course, come morning we would have to take our quilts and fold them and put them away.

We had so many things to look forward to – like the ripening of the grapes. We had a grape arbor that had to be a hundred feet long. It had two long lines of grapes that crossed over the top. The vines made a

50

long tunnel. It was such a joy to sit on the ground and eat all the grapes we could pick and that our stomachs could handle. From experience, we knew not to eat the green ones. Lots of things you learn on the farm that nobody has to teach you. Mother Nature does that for you.

Toward the end of summer, it was possible to find a hidden watermelon patch that had gotten covered by the cotton. You could bust a melon and eat it right there. Or you could go to the garden, get a turnip, peel it and eat it raw. In the fall, you could sit under the pecan trees and eat pecans to your heart's content. There was always something pleasurable to do. Or at least for me there was.

One of the most wonderful times was in the winter when we came home from school and Mama would have a pot of hominy on the big wooden stove. It didn't happen too often because it was a lot of trouble. It had been cooking most of the day. Oh, how good it tasted. Nowhere in the world can you find hominy as good as that, straight from the kettle.

We made a big platter of candy every day. Sometimes we would even make divinity. We all knew how to make fudge. That was routine at our house.

In the fall when the fruit became ripe, the orchard was a favorite place to visit. We spent time under the fruit trees. We had apple, pear, plum and peach trees, and many pecan trees. We had two persimmon trees; if you ate them before they ripened, they made your mouth pucker.

When the corn had all been gathered, you could take the stalks and make a teepee out of them. When the hay had been baled and put in the barn in layers like a stairstep, that was magic in itself. We had a rope with a pulley on it. I suppose it was to get the bales up to the top. Wow! that was like a trapeze to us. We could swing from the highest bale and as far out as we chose and down to the bottom row. What a delight!

At Christmas time, Mama baked and baked. She put the pies in the china cabinet. I remember once there were 58 pies and 18 cakes. When you got a piece of pie, it was a fourth of a pie, not an eighth! She always had a baked ham – it was a whole ham – and she decorated it beautifully.

Once I was sitting on a bench at the table. She was using both the bench and the table to make two big pans of fruit salad. They looked so good. I got a little restless and wiggled the bench. Mama warned me not to turn the bench over. She probably should have made me move, because I wiggled again and over went the pans of fruit salad. I doubt if I got spanked. Mama only spanked when she was in the mood. Then everyone got it, even if it had been a while since they had acted up. We knew how to scatter at those times. Maybe we did not get all the training that the earlier kids had, but I was sure happy with my place in the family by then. I really do not feel that I had much unhappiness at all.

The Storm Cellar

Mama wanted a storm cellar. When she lacked a helper for a project, she did it herself. She managed to dig out the area and make a form for the concrete. She mixed her own cement in a wheelbarrow, mixed some iron with it and spread it heavily over the form. That storm cellar was *very* strong. However, next year when Bud started looking for parts for the cultivator, he found they had been used in the storm cellar cement, along with a few other pieces of iron from other farm equipment. Mama got her storm cellar, all right, and many nights we went there. Papa would not always go in during a storm, but when he did, we knew we were in for a big one.

One of the times Betty and her kids were visiting, it was stormy, so they stayed close to the storm cellar in case the weather got worse. In fact, it did get worse; they went into the storm cellar, and then suddenly remembered Aunt Annie who lived right next door. Betty opened the door a crack and saw Aunt Annie trying to get there. Her body was so thin; her clothes were blowing backwards from the strong turbulent winds and she could not go any farther. Betty said, "I have to go help her." Betty's kids were crying and hanging on to her so tight for fear she would get blown away. Betty pushed them back and took off to get Aunt Annie. She reached her, grabbed her by the arms and started dragging her to the storm cellar. Those looking on said Aunt Annie's feet never touched the ground after Betty got hold of her until they reached the cellar. After they got in and sat down, and Aunt Annie began to get her breath back, she gasped, "I declare, Betty, you have jerked the crick right out of my back."

When the storm finally cleared and they all came out to daylight, Mama lost it. She saw her crops were completely gone. Betty said Mama was confused for a little while, but they had weathered the storm. That year, there was no financial gain.

Pauline and Bob

Pauline was 14 when she met Bob Henderson. She was playing basketball and Bob was coaching. She dated several guys throughout the years, and she could have had almost anyone, but Bob was always the one. It just took her a while to get him. Actually, she dated two Bobs. Bob Forsyth was the other. They each had their regular nights.

On one occasion, when Pauline was due to have her regular date with the right Bob, a guy showed up from out of town that she wanted to go out with. This created a dilemma because, without a phone, there was no quick way to break a date. Her best reasoning was to have Mary Lee tell Bob Henderson she had to leave and would contact him later. Bob arrived, walking into the house in his self-confident way, ignoring Mary Lee, as usual, and not really listening to the explanation for Pauline's absence. He walked over, grabbed the newspaper and sat down to read until Pauline appeared. We had no closets in those days; we hung a pole in the corner of the room for hanging clothes, and another pole for a curtain to cover them with. Meanwhile, in the bedroom behind the curtain, amid the clothes, Pauline stood waiting for Mary Lee to convince Bob she was not there. After a bit, Bob decided Mary Lee might have been serious. He got up, went to the bedroom door and looked in. Just then, the curtain and all the clothes fell at Pauline's feet, leaving her completely exposed. All she could say was, "Oh, I was looking for something different to wear." She came walking over the clothes, greeted Bob as if nothing had happened, and left with him for their date. So Virginia had to entertain the guy from out of town. With that many girls in one house, sometimes our dates overlapped.

I remember the other Bob that was so in love with Pauline. He was always bringing her something, something usually cute and interesting. Once he brought some gum for Mike. Mike took it and started chewing. Pauline, encouraging Mike to show manners, said "Now Mike, what do you say?" Mike had a bad stutter. He said something like the following: "Dooo yoyou haahave aanother another piece for Mama?" It was easy to see where his loyalties lay.

Virginia was always jealous of the chosen Bob. She tolerated him for the nine years that Pauline was dating him, but it all came to a head when Mr. and Mrs. Bob Henderson returned from their honeymoon. The newlyweds were supposed to stay with Bob's parents while their apartment was being finished. Incredibly, the very day of their return, a faulty flue in the Henderson home caused a fire and their house burned to the ground. No one was harmed, but it was a total loss. Someone asked Pauline where they were going to stay. Virginia butted in, "Pauline's coming home where she belongs." Pauline did come home – with Bob – as a short term solution. More specifically, they moved their things into

54

the bedroom that Virginia and Pauline had shared. I don't know where Virginia was intended to sleep, but when bedtime came, she didn't hesitate – she climbed into bed next to Pauline. The next night, Pauline slept with Virginia, and Bob went to stay with his sister.

Rural Electrification Act (R.E.A.)

The R.E.A. folks had wired our whole house, getting it ready for the electricity to be turned on. We were just getting it in the country; the city had its electricity already.

Bob Forsyth found out that our electricity was due to come on just before Christmas. He also knew we had the Christmas tree ready to go up. His next night out with Pauline, he brought her lights for the tree. They spent the evening decorating the Christmas tree in hope that the electricity would actually come on in time for Christmas. Never having electricity before, we were overjoyed at the thought of a lit tree.

As it turned out, they didn't come on before Christmas, but a short time after. When the moment came, Mama was in the living room intent on something else, and WHAM – the whole living room lit up. Mama threw her arms up as if something had attacked her and started running before she realized what had happened. It was the best Christmas tree we ever had. And what a wonderful thing to have electric lights in every room. Carrying a lamp around was a thing of the past.

Not only did we have electric lights, we also had an electric pump that pumped the water into the house. We actually had running water in the sink; even better, we were set up for bathroom conveniences. We would have water in the bathtub and sink and a commode that flushed. The whole family was ecstatic over such luxury. Not a washtub bath or a sponge bath, but a real *bathtub* bath. No more Sears and Roebuck catalogs in the outhouse. Just plain old toilet paper. We didn't even have to catch rain water to wash our hair in. That was pure happiness.

Grandma Perry

In 1935, Grandma Perry, Mom's mother, became ill. She had moved to town by then and we younger kids got to know her a little better. She had always seemed to be so happy to see Aunt Annie's children but kind of held back with us. Maryan Ruth says she remembers Grandma reaching out to her many times, probably because she had lost her mother when Mike was born.

I do not remember ever visiting her before she moved to town. I think maybe there was jealousy involved. Papa had bought her land, and we had so much more. Whatever the case, Mama was there for her when she was so sick. As her condition began to get worse, Mama never left her side. In her last hours, when she was barely conscious, she began to mutter things about the past. The very last words she spoke were... Edgar, Edgar. She repeated his name twice before she slipped into her afterlife, leaving everyone believing that she was seeing Edgar, her long lost son. Maybe they both made it home. Anna Eddings Ray Perry died October 11, 1935.

Lloyd

We had a pump that had stopped producing water. Lloyd worked really hard to drive a new pump, but there was no water to be had at that location. He became so frustrated that he took the shotgun and shot down the well. Bingo! The shot ricocheted and went in his leg instead of the well. Just Lloyd's luck. He seemed to create enough excitement for the whole household.

Lloyd did like the girls. A new family moved into our part of the country. He asked Virginia and Pauline to invite them over for dinner on Sunday. They were Hazel and Daisy Thornton and both were very attractive girls. Being new in town, they were excited to be invited to our house. They had heard a lot about the Mooney girls. They went to the library and checked out an Emily Post to study before coming to our house. That was a joke. Try to have good manners with that many children of all ages. By the time the last ones came along, we just fended for ourselves. The girls remained our friends and eventually married local boys.

More of Mama's Projects

Mama decided she needed to increase her kitchen space. No one seemed to be interested but Mama. She wanted to take out a wall that would make the kitchen much bigger. Papa needed to settle and just be comfortable. Mama waited for Papa and Lloyd to go to town. She took a handsaw, an axe, a crowbar and a sledge hammer and started to work on that stupid wall that was in her way. She had the wall half down when the men returned from their business trip. Papa took one look at the mess that Mama had made, never showing agitation. All he said was, "Oh Wife, you need help; you shouldn't have." Then he went to the field and recruited some farm hands to convert into carpenters, who then finished the job.

At another time, Mama wanted some concrete steps in front of the house and decided to build them herself. She used a wheelbarrow and acquired fresh gravel from the road for the concrete. She would send some of the kids out to the road whenever she needed more. Knowing she was overstepping her bounds a little, she would say, "Now don't get any if a car comes by." When she finished, she had sturdy concrete steps with banisters.

Bud and Pansy

Bud was the next to get married. His girlfriend was Pansy Evans, a very serious girl and a good person. Bud was serious too in those days. Even though he was too young for marriage, he truly loved Pansy. She, at 19, was older and mature enough for marriage. They married and he was a good husband for a few years. He worked and cleared the land that Papa had given them. Hard work was the name of the game when it came to clearing ground.

Very soon they started their family. First, they had a little boy they named Gene, then another boy they named Jimmy. Sometime afterward, Pansy went to work in a grocery store to help out. Bud, thinking it would lighten the load for himself and Pansy, moved them to the farm close to Mama.

Helping the Kids

Papa saw his married children struggling to make a living. Since he was in better shape financially, he decided to help them as he had helped Bud. Papa also bought land in the new ground (meaning land that needed to be cleared) for Lloyd and similar land around Poplar Bluff for Stella and Kirb. He bought land for Anna and Clarence and Willie and Doc in other areas. However, he was not financially able to continue this practice for the younger children.

Problems with Lloyd

Lloyd married a fine young lady named Lola Hudson. Lloyd was not a steady person; he had lots of hang ups, and he caused Mama and Papa much grief. He drank too much and ran around with people who enjoyed the same way of life. Lola was dismayed. Mama and Papa tried to make up the difference with Lola for Lloyd's lack of attention. At one time, Lloyd and his friends were out drinking and driving and ran into a big ditch and wrecked the car. Tony Tucker, who had been driving Lloyd's car, was killed. He was married with a family. That was a stressful time for us.

Lloyd had an Indian motorcycle. He rode it up and down the gravel road at top speed in front of our house, always angry at himself for his behavior, but taking it out on Papa. He wrecked the motorcycle once, broke his leg, and was permanently crippled. Of course, Papa came to his rescue. Along about then, Lloyd's health began to fail.

Arizona

One summer, Papa bought a house trailer and planned a trip to Arizona, hoping the dry air would improve Lloyd's health. Come fall, he and Lloyd took off to spend the winter in Arizona. Lloyd did most of the driving. Mama and Papa had always considered that their kids were good drivers. Lloyd proved them wrong. Three months later on the trip home, they drove into a gas station to fill up; in leaving, Lloyd took the whole gas tank with him. Papa never seemed to get shook up. He just took care of any damages and drove on. They made it safely home, but with a car and trailer showing some wear.

When Papa drove up after his long trip, I rushed over to hug him. I then became very conscious of my clothes, because I was wearing a pair of short shorts. We were not allowed to wear short shorts. After a big welcome, I ran in to change. We had been playing tennis on our new tennis court that had been made for us in his absence.

The house trailer was put to good use even after the trip. The smaller kids were allowed to sleep in it at night, which was a big adventure. One night I was sleeping in there along with one of the other kids. Even though we were parked close to the house, it was kind of scary. This one particular night, I was lying there awake, when I heard the door knob turn and the door rattled a little bit. I knew immediately it was a prowler, and I was frightened. A few nights before, I had heard someone in the chicken house, and knew they were stealing chickens because of their squawking as they were being caught. I listened, thinking of what to do if the prowler opened the door. I decided to make him think there was an adult in there instead of kids. And the solution was right there, just what I needed, a big pair of boots. I picked them up and raised them as high as my arm would take them and dropped them on the floor. All of a sudden, I heard someone outside run over some buckets that had been left by the vehicle. I think I scared him as bad as he scared me.

Papa Getting Older

Papa was getting older, less active and staying in more, and Mama was beginning to take over the farm, but under Papa's direction. Mama was still full of vitality, being 25 years younger then Papa. She managed very well. Papa still bought his new Dodge every year, even though the kids did most of the driving. They contributed a few dents along the way, as well.

When Papa had to go to town on business, he wore his very worst clothes, I think so people would not know he was prosperous. But he was not fooling anyone. The very funny thing is that he had a reputation of having more money than he actually had.

Most of his business was conducted in the living room. People came to him. We were trained not to go through the front of the house when Papa had a business person there. That applied to most of us that paid attention, but it did not seem to apply to Mary Lee. One day after school, she went barreling through the living room. Papa said to her, "Daughter, have you not heard that old saying?" What he meant was: children should be seen and not heard. Papa raised us on clichés. Now

Mary Lee was always fast with the answers. Her reply to him was, "Sure Pop, speak now or forever hold your peace." We respected him so much, raising us had to be easy on his part. Of course, you have to give Mama the real credit for making it easy for him.

Papa had a birthday. We all knew it, and we knew Mama did not give gifts on birthdays. I think to many of us, not giving gifts made it harder, because we wanted to show our affection. This birthday impressed me so much. I really felt that I had to do something. I went over to Freeman's Store and bought a box of cigars for Papa and then charged it to him. When he smoked, it was cigars. I did not know he had quit smoking again. He was never a heavy smoker anyway. I took this box of cigars home and went to his room where he usually stayed. He was sitting in his chair, and Betty was brushing his thin white hair. I lovingly gave him the cigars and wished him a happy birthday. He looked at me with such tender love, making me think I had done the most wonderful thing in the world. His words were, "Oh daughter, thank you; you did not have to do that." Never once did he say that he had quit smoking, nor did he ask where I got the money. He knew that I had none, and he knew it went on his charge.

He really was as special as we all thought he was. I could have gotten a scolding, but what I got was a special memory that stays with me even now. Those cigars sat by his chair unopened for a long time in a place of honor.

Deaths

Too Many Funerals. Not long after Papa's birthday, Lola and Lloyd had a baby. It had a damaged heart from the beginning and only lived six months. After the baby died, Lola left Lloyd and went home. Lloyd became sicker and was put to bed in our house. He lived six months, and he died. Lloyd was buried in the family graveyard. I stayed home with Papa during Lloyd's funeral. The funeral procession had to pass our house to get to the cemetery. Papa sat in his chair with his head on his walking cane, watching as the long line of cars passed the house, with big tears rolling down his cheeks. I felt devastated not knowing how to comfort Papa, so I cried with him.

About six months later, Papa died, on February 21, 1940. Now you have to know after three deaths what kind of shape Mama was in. It was a mournful time for a while. Mama just sat and listened to sad music and cried. It was almost more than we could stand. She had weathered many storms, never really breaking, but not this time. The rest of us bounced back, but not Mama.

A Cruel Joke. About three months later, Betty and Maryan Ruth and I decided to give Pauline and Virginia a big scare. We were inspired by our Halloween activities a few months back; the school had had a graveyard in one of the booths, with epitaphs on the headstones. This was in October before Papa died. We did not even consider the effect our prank could have on those still suffering from the shock of too many funerals so close together. We were young and resilient.

We took Pauline's cedar chest and put it on two chairs at the foot of the bed. We raised the lid up, took a white sheet and draped it over the back and into the would-be casket, and made it look real by adding a pillow or two with white pillowcases. We scrunched up the pillows to make it look like a covered body. Bob Forsyth had given Pauline a beautiful ship's light that cast an eerie blue glow. We turned that on and the other lights off so we could get that special effect over the makeshift casket. This was the very room that Papa had been laid out in for viewing. His body was kept there four days and nights before his funeral. People, mostly neighbors, had sat up all night with his body, as was the custom in those days.

We made it look like the real thing. Pauline and Virginia came in together that night from their dates and went directly to their bedroom. Their bedroom was one of the front rooms with a window in the door. They got to the door and looked through the window in shock and opened the door. Then and there, Pauline passed out. Can you believe how much trouble we got in? Just over a trick. We really had Halloween in mind, not death, just pretending. It was the working of immature minds.

Farming with a Vengeance

When Mama began to come alive again, she took over farming with a vengeance. We all went to work. It was so good to have Mama back in action. She had plenty of hands to do the field work. We were busy either weighing the cotton or taking it to the gin. Mary Lee and I both knew how to hook up the trailer full of cotton and drive it to the gin. It was put on the scales to be weighed and then the cotton was sucked out of the trailer to be processed. That kept us pretty busy. We all felt productive. Mama was the glue that held us together and we began to feel happy again.

We had an incubator that held 200 eggs. Those eggs were marked on one side, and they had to be turned every day until they hatched. When the eggs hatched out, Mama would have us take the unhatched eggs to the field and clean out the trays of the incubator. Sometimes a day or two later, a few baby chickens would find their way back to the yard; the warm sun made them hatch out.

We had many more chickens than we could possibly use. Once when I asked for a pair of roller skates, Mama had me gather the eggs, take them to town and sell them, and then she would get me the skates. That she did. She ordered the skates for me. I feel it might have been a way to teach me how to manage my finances.

A roadster with a rumble seat that had belonged to Lloyd and an A-Model of Bud's were available for us to drive. One day, we decided to use the roadster to go to the movies. No one freely handed out money for such things; therefore, we had to come up with some money ourselves. It would have been about a quarter apiece to get in. Mama never objected to us going to the movies and went quite often herself. The movie was in Blytheville, about ten miles away. To foot the bill, we went out and caught four old hens, which were no problem to sell. We put the chickens in the rumble seat of the roadster and started to back out. We had not asked permission to catch the chickens, but we had at least a hundred running around outside the house and barn. Mama called my name; she needed something from town. I walked over to the screened-in front porch to see what she wanted. She gave me money for her purchases, and as I was walking away, the chickens started squawking. A dead giveaway. I glanced back at Mama just in time to see her turn away with a slight smile on her face.

Bud and the R.E.A.

Bud had sold his farm and and was farming and living on some of Papa's land. It was months after we got electricity that a collector called on him about three months' of overdue light bills. Bud was shocked. Everyone knew that farmers did their financial thing in the spring or fall. Stunned, he just stood there looking at the collector. The young man said to Bud, "You have to pay this bill or we will cut off your lights." Bud, being a man of few – but strong – words, said to the astonished collector, "Do you see that bulldozer out there? Do you see all those light poles on this 400 acres of land? Well, if you turn off my electricity, I will take that bulldozer and push down every light pole on this place." The poor guy left not knowing what to do. I might add that Bud paid his electric bill monthly after that.

Helping Aunt Annie

Aunt Annie and her husband Charlie Marrs had fallen on hard times and needed a place to live. This was mainly due to Charlie's lack of ambition for labor of any kind. He was a Justice of the Peace and dabbled in court work some, but he was getting old and not able to do so much. Mama came to the rescue. She had a carpenter convert the commissary into an apartment. It was practically in our backyard. That was a good thing, because not long afterward, Charley died and left Aunt Annie alone. Aunt Annie needed us. She did not drive and always needed to go somewhere.

A New Driver

Mama needed a driver for the car, but no one was available to take her. I don't know why Mama was so unsure of her driving, but she was, and would not drive unless desperate. This was her desperate day. She decided to take herself over to town. She was confident about most things but not driving. So she backed the car out of the driveway and slowly took off. Town was only a mile away, but you had to cross an old iron bridge. It was protected by iron sides and had planks as a track for the car to drive on. Somehow, Mama got off the tracks and swiped the side of the bridge, ripping open the whole length of the brand new black Dodge. That was the end of her driving – and that's why we all learned to drive. I think Papa should have kept an old car around for Mama to wreck.

Eventually, I was the one next in line for lessons. Mama showed me how by driving up and down the driveway twice. Then she put me in the driver's seat. She showed me the brake first, next the clutch and shift. There was no such thing as an automatic. I guess steering was not important in her mind and was not part of the lesson. On my first trip out of the drive, I backed all the way across the road and into the ditch.

Fortunately, the ditch was dry so I could drive out of it. The lesson was over. I was good to go. After a few trips to town, Mama had a new experienced driver who was thrilled to know how to drive.

Mama got up bright and early one morning and informed me that I was to drive her to Poplar Bluff. Wow!! I did not feel *that* brave, but since I was not willing to give up my new-found driving job, I packed my bag ready to go. Stella lived in Poplar Bluff. She and Mama were very close. Maybe Stella, who was the oldest, understood her better than the rest. Mama had 13 kids and Stella had 12. I am sure they had a certain amount of commonality.

All the way to Poplar Bluff, the highway was just a narrow two-lane road. I hung on to that steering wheel like it might get away, and Mama sat back with her eyes closed, whistling a song that had no tune. What a relief – we made it. I had lots of fun with my cousins for a few days until it was time to return. It was easier going back. Happy, happy I was. Now I could go anywhere and use the car whenever I got ready.

Mama thought 80 miles an hour was average because most of us drove that speed. There was not very much traffic in those days, though. She would just sit there and whistle, just happy to be going somewhere. Since Papa was not around anymore, she went a lot; a driver was very important to her.

The state said you needed a driver's license to be legit. Thus eventually, Mama went to Blytheville to the courthouse and paid fifty cents for a legal driver's license for me. I had already driven a few years with no driver's license needed until now. I do not remember ever having to watch my speed, either. None of us ever got a speeding ticket.

Betty

Betty, being the baby, did not get into much trouble and was also spoiled. The truth is, she had been special to Papa and got more attention than me. She spent most of her time on the arm of Papa's chair. She sat there and brushed his hair or hugged him or just talked to him. She really was Papa's baby. She would ask, "Papa, sing me a song." He sometimes sang our favorite song: "The daring young man on the flying trapeze. He flew through the air with the greatest of ease." I think when he sang that song, he felt it all the way through. His eyes would twinkle, his shoulders would sway, with a slight smile upon his lips. We all thrilled to see him in such a mellow mood.

Betty began to grow up. She was not yet ready for driving, but I'm not sure she knew that. One day when Louise was visiting, Betty asked if she would like to go with her to Manila. A group of the young boys had gone swimming at the lake in Manila. Louise, a little younger than Betty, of course said yes. That was the wrong answer, because Betty could not drive. Betty informed Louise, "The car is sitting there with the keys in it." No one ever took the keys out, at our house anyway; they would surely have gotten lost.

Betty and Louise took off for Manila. Betty wasn't sure what gear she was in. Untrained though she was, she made it over Big Lake and turned toward the dam. But when they arrived, everyone had gone. To head back home, they needed to turn around, but Betty didn't know how to make the car go backwards. Their ingenious solution was to take down a fence so they could circle around instead of backing up; then they could head for home in a straight shot. They did make the circle, but in doing so, they got stuck in some ruts. They did not know enough to get the car out, so they started walking home. It was getting late, and it was at least an eight-mile walk. When it was almost dark, a car stopped to pick them up. The principal of our school – of all people – opened the door and ordered the two girls to get in. He gave them a scolding they would remember, about what happens to young girls when they are out at night unchaperoned. Now this was the guy you had to answer to at school. After the lecture, he took them home for their parents to deal with.

Pansy's Revenge

Bud developed a wild hair after 5 or 6 years of marriage. It did not help that he had married at 17. He was getting involved with other females, one in particular. Poor Pansy was a very good girl and wanted only Bud. We all loved her and felt bad for her.

Bud had acquired a taste for adventure and excitement. I'm afraid that I might have had a little of that in me also; otherwise, I would not have agreed to go along with Pansy's somewhat crazy idea. She wanted to try getting herself out of the locked trunk of her car, for a reason I didn't understand until later. We went down this lonely road for her tryout. She found that she could indeed get out of the trunk on her own. Thank goodness, that was the end of my services. However, I sensed Bud was in for trouble.

Pansy knew he was going out that night, so she set up her trap. Unbeknownst to Bud, before he left the house, Pansy had climbed into the trunk of the car. Bud took off on his adventure; he picked up the girl he was seeing – her name was Marie – and off they went. As I understood it, Bud had this eerie feeling along the way that he was being watched or being followed. He was feeling uncomfortable. He finally pulled the car over to the side of the road and just sat there, feeling uneasy.

Pansy went into action. She jumped out of the trunk, went to the driver's side and demanded that Bud scoot over. In total shock, he did exactly that. My goodness, my goodness, he and Marie got the ride of their lives. They went down that two-lane narrow highway at breakneck speed. Pansy was putting all her vengeance into that wild ride. In fear for their lives, Bud finally decided he had to take control. He first demanded that she stop the car and was utterly ignored. Not realizing he was doing something just as dangerous, he reached over and turned off the ignition key. When he did that, it locked the wheels and they all went into a ditch. He took over the driving from there. Before he could deal with Pansy, he had to take Marie home.

Pansy and Bud parted company after that. Gene chose to live with his dad. I think he liked excitement also.

Maryan Ruth

A New Skirt. Mary Lee had gone to work at a general store. She had her own money and wanted her privacy – a place to call her own. So she took a dressing table and, with her own money, bought material to put a skirt around it to use as her own personal makeup table. She took pins and pleated it and then tacked it around the table. It looked very nice.

That night Maryan Ruth wanted something new to wear. After Mary Lee had gone, she took the new skirt off the table and turned it into a new skirt for herself. As luck would have it, we all ended up at the same place that night. Much to Mary Lee's horror, in walked Maryan Ruth wearing Mary Lee's dressing table skirt. Talk about a real upset. Well, that was it. Mad, Mary Lee was.

Ten girls were a lot to handle. With Maryan Ruth, that made eleven. Mama had to be a saint.

High Spirited. We had horses but only one Virginia roan. She was a truly spirited riding horse. Even though Papa warned us about her, every chance Marion Ruth got, she would sneak her out and ride her. Maryan Ruth was almost as spirited as the horse. One day she was over at town and this young boy was trying to flirt with her. Maryan Ruth just kind of ignored him and he felt injured. He took his foot and kicked Brownie right in the flanks. Well, Brownie took off flying, Maryan Ruth hanging on for dear life, going right down the main street of Dell. She kept yelling, "Stop her, stop her, and her name is Brownie." Well, Brownie finally stopped on her own. This experience, however, did not stop Maryan Ruth from sneaking off with Brownie whenever she could.

I think Maryan Ruth – like Brownie – was a little more spirited than I was. I may have had a milder disposition; more likely, I did not like to reveal my true nature in public.

Getting Even. Maryan Ruth, on the other hand, would pick a fight with me in front of anybody. Mostly, I would keep my mouth shut. However, everyone does get their day and my day was in math class. Math was really my thing in school. On one occasion, the teacher assigned our lesson for the next day and I went home to study. I really worked hard on that whole lesson, but there was one problem I just could not get. Next day at school, Mr. Mullins, our teacher, asked if anyone had a problem with the homework. I held up my hand and told him I just could not get number 13. He told me – and the whole class – that 13 was beyond what he had assigned and then went into a whole tale of me being a good student and really trying. Maryan Ruth, who was in the same class and maybe a little jealous of the attention, spoke up, "Oh, she just planned that to get your attention." Of course I was embarrassed, but the teacher defended me. Then he gave us our next assignment.

In class the next day, Mr. Mullins picked out certain problems and asked for them to be put on the blackboard. He assigned number 9 for Maryan Ruth. Now I was well acquainted with how Maryan Ruth displayed her work on the blackboard. She would put the right answer (from the back of the book) at the end of the problem and fill in any old figures to get to the answer.

Mr. Mullins asked, "Does anyone need any problem explained?" Now was my chance; I sweetly asked, "Will you have number 9 explained, please?" His question, "Who has number 9?" Maryan Ruth could not explain it because she had not worked it. Mr. Mullins and the whole class knew what went on. We all had a big laugh over that, which is all the punishment she got.

Vida and Haywood

There was a strong bond uniting the ten sisters. If something happened to one, it usually happened to nine more; we were always that close in our upbringing. We hugged, we cried, we all mourned together. We hung close.

Vida came in from her date one night. We were all sitting on the screened-in porch. It was a nice warm night and we were enjoying a cool breeze. Haywood let her out of the car and he drove off. Vida informed everyone that she and Haywood had married a few days earlier. She was about 17. What an explosive reaction she got from her older sisters! They carried on like it was a disgrace. Mary Lee just went berserk. I could kind of understand Mary Lee's reaction; the two were so close. Mama and Papa did not say a word; they were kind about it, understanding the newlyweds' need for acceptance. They happily welcomed Haywood into the family. In about an hour, Haywood came back and took Vida home with him.

In truth, their marriage was never a mistake. They were always extremely happy in their life together. The girls calmed down after a few days and got over the loss of another sister. Vida was able to enjoy her new status after that.

Bud Ruins the Day

Once I spent the whole summer with my sister Johnnie who lived in Saint Louis, Missouri. While I was there, I became infatuated with a guy and we dated until it was time to return home. After a few months, he asked if he could ride down and see me. Johnnie came with him. I was working the day he was supposed to arrive. I had worked hard to get the house clean and make things look good.

While I was at work, my brother Bud had bought a new spray gun, or – I should say – new toy. He talked Mama into letting him spray her dining room walls. I came in from work, took one look and just sat down and cried. Not only had he sprayed the walls, he had sprayed the china cabinet, the buffet, and anything else that got in the way. There was no way in such a short time that I could make it right. I threw a fit.

Mama usually took things calmly, but I could be emotional; and she had a hard time with me when I was. When the guy arrived, I apologized for the extra paint. Soon after he went back to the city, I forgot him anyway. This was just one of Bud's stunts. I did not quit loving Bud in spite of his many stunts.

Sharing Bud's Adventures

That was not the end of Bud's adventures. Next thing he did was take flying lessons. Then he bought a plane. I believe he was a good pilot. He had to be or he would never have survived all that he put that plane through. He also bought a Harley Davidson motorcycle. I was about 15 at the time and wanted to do everything Bud was doing. First I asked to learn to ride the bike. Bud took me down the road once and brought me back – two miles maybe. Then I was on my own. He neglected to tell me about the clutch. I got on the bike, put my feet where they belonged and turned the controls a little. The clutch slipped and I was on my way. I looked back for help; what I got was "Keep going – you're own your own." I went down the road and did not know how to turn it around so I did so manually. I made it back fine and that was my lesson. Lack of instruction never stopped me; we took many trips on the Harley.

Flying Lessons

I also asked for a flying lesson. Unbeknownst to me, Bud told everyone he was going to scare me to death. Did I learn anything from the lesson? No. What can you learn when you're in a tailspin? Or in a loop, upside down? Or in a stall? A stall is when the nose of the plane goes straight up and flops down. You are going down and your stomach is still going up. Well, that was my first lesson. Second lesson: Take off fast and high. We had our own airfield – a forty-acre pasture, with tall trees right at the end of the field. When I landed, I bounced a few feet up and down all the way to the end of the runway.

Since I did not know my way around from the air, I learned that I had better follow the highway. Now if I had had a teacher instead of a daredevil, I would have done well. Even though Bud was more interested in scaring me than teaching me, I did not quit. I went through three planes with him. I owned one-third of the third plane, only because he was short of money.

One of the things Bud did was to keep Mama's field hands running for cover. He often greeted his spectators with a nose dive just to say hello. Poor Aunt Annie was so frightened of the plane, when she heard it over the field, she ran for it. Bud was putting a lot of things to test in those years. I enjoyed all of his adventures. How could I fault him when I wanted to learn the very things he was doing.

We had a regular weekend place to hang out. In addition to our own private airport, we had a grandstand made of hay bales to sit on. We had family that gathered there every weekend for fun and plane rides. It *was* great fun. Gene and Mike were passengers every time they got a chance. On one of those trips, Bud was returning from taking Gene for a ride. When he turned the plane to head home, he heard a big pop. Bud did not know what it was, so he decided to bring the plane straight down instead of maneuvering to the regular field. As he was coming in for a landing, Gene – who was six – reached up, touched his dad's shoulder and calmly asked, "Are you going to make it, Dad?" His dad's reply was, "Yes, son, we will make it fine," which they did. The plane got a few wounds, though, since they came down in a cornfield, but it got repaired and the fun continued.

One Sunday afternoon, Bud was taking Gene and Mike for a ride. He was using the field just across the road from the house. They were in the plane getting ready for a takeoff. Our dog, Master, was upset because Bud had the little boys in the plane with him. Master came from our front yard and started barking at the plane. The dog was aggressively trying to stop the plane! Still barking furiously, he ran into the propellers. It knocked his jaws completely sideways. The dog accomplished his mission, but he had to be put to sleep. That upset us all. We loved that dog. It also ended the flying for that day.

When Bud wasn't giving people rides, he was still teaching me to fly – and still trying to scare me. However, I trusted him and thought he knew what he was doing. I could take off – very fast – over that clump of trees at the end of our field. I could do a tailspin and a stall and a few other unusual things, although I knew nothing about how to fly from Blytheville to Dell except to follow the highway. Both our fields were too short to be a proper airstrip, even though one was 40 acres; it was wider than longer. I was still having bumpy landings.

Mary Lee and Buford

Mary Lee had been dating Buford Jarrett. He was an accomplished, handsome gentleman. He was already into farming his family land. One morning she awoke, found Mama and said, "I am getting married." Then she burst into tears, much to Mama's surprise. Mama did not know whether to congratulate her or give her a handkerchief. My opinion is that Mary Lee had fallen for a guy that was not good husband material and was trying to get over him when she started dating Buford. But she also knew a good catch when she saw him. Whatever the case, she loved Buford and they had a good life together.

When they had been married eight years and still had no babies, they adopted a six-month old girl and named her Melody. After a few more years, Mary Lee finally got pregnant and gave birth to a girl, Sandra, and then a boy, Calvin Buford "Jerry" Jarrett.

My family was close to Mary Lee and her family. We were living in California by then, but we spent time with them on our yearly vacations.

World War II

On December 7, 1941, Japan attacked and nearly destroyed Pearl Harbor. That got us into World War II. Then the whole world changed. I was 17 years old. It was strange; for weeks before the attack, I was having these terrible dreams. Once I dreamed a big plane was going over the ocean, and the wings of the plane were loaded with men with guns. I had many more similar dreams. When war was declared, I quit dreaming of all those planes going over the ocean. I guess because they really were.

We were like sitting ducks in Pearl Harbor. Our planes were old, and our military was not up to par. That changed, though; almost overnight, it seemed, everything was converted to support the war effort. The planes evolved from propellers to jets.

Deprivations. For us at home, there were no new cars, no silk stockings. You cannot believe what the first nylons felt like – terrible, they would not stay up, they wrinkled on your legs. What a disaster. Gas was rationed. The car we used had a leaky gas tank, so we kept a big bar of yellow soap in the car to stop the leaks. We used the motorcycle for most of our trips. Thank goodness for our motorcycle; it did not take much gas. Sugar was rationed among many other things. However, we did not feel the hardships so much, because we were on a farm and had most of what we needed. Cigarettes were also rationed and I did smoke at that time, as it was the fashionable thing to do. Lucky for me that I had a retailer that kind of looked out for me.

When Mary Lee, Betty and I got ready to go out of town, we would put Betty on the bus with our suitcase and Mary Lee and I would take off on the motorcycle. We were usually going to Vida's; she lived on the airbase where Haywood, her husband, worked. Our local airbase was quickly turned into a SAC base, where young cadets were trained to become pilots. The law of eminent domain had gone into effect fast. Land was taken for airbases. Factories were switched over to making war materials. Women learned to do things that had been handled by men before the war.

Most of the local guys were gone to fight. One of our friends was among the very first guys to be called and did not come back until after the war. His name was Jay Ashbranner. I remember so well because I had a big crush on him. He felt deprived because so many locally stationed G.I.s got to go on furloughs when he was overseas fighting. By the time he came back, I had a crush on someone else.

All Doing Our Part. Most of our friends were drafted, but everyone went to war, one way or another. If you were a farmer, you were classified 4F, meaning you did not have to go to war, because food was all-important for the armed forces. We girls did our best to entertain the troops. Life moved fast and things happened that would not have at a quieter time. The very first soldiers were housed in the armory building until the barracks could be built. Once, when we took one of the soldiers home to the armory, we told him we would be back later on the motorcycle. He and his friends just laughed at us, not believing it. Accepting that as a challenge, Mary Lee and I went home, got on the motorcycle and drove back up just to show them. Of course I was the driver.

We were all frightened and also a little giddy, as an emergency will make you. We were on the fast track in just about everything: fun, worry, excitement and fear.

There was a group of cadets that we met in town quite often. On one particular day, we were to meet the group at a certain place in Blytheville. On our way to Blytheville, which was ten miles from where we lived, we started watching a plane in the air. It was acting strange. We stopped the car to see better. Finally, the plane went down too low for us to see, but we were concerned. We knew these were just young boys learning to fly. The guys were late getting to our destination. When they arrived, they all seemed upset. The plane had gone down, and in it were two of our friends in the group. They were learning to do maneuvers and something went wrong. Those two never made it to fight in the war.

Once I went with Mary Lee to Tallahassee, Florida where Buford was. That is when I found out how scarce hotel rooms were. The armed forces took priority – as it should be – but that meant we did not have a place to stay. We sat in the lobby for hours before we could find a place to sleep. It made us careful about planning trips in the future. Travel was limited to bus and train; civilian air travel only became possible later.

I fell madly in love with a young corporal stationed in Newport, the town where Vida and Haywood lived. He was from Alabama. We spent many weekends going to Newport. So many letters I wrote to Corporal Alfred J. McClinton. Just his name would bring tingles to my skin. He sent me perfume from Paris, which I shared with my sisters. My feelings were so strong for him, but I was a little uncertain about the outcome of our relationship. Being a time of war, emotions ran high.

Alfred wrote me that his brother had been sent to a hospital in Memphis and asked me to go see him. I made arrangements for Pansy to go with me. We were walking the corridor to his brother's room and coming to meet us was… Alfred! with a cute nurse on each arm. You can imagine my reaction. He had lately been sent back to the states and was visiting his brother. I truly was in shock, but somehow I seemed to know that my love was stronger than his. When he returned to his home in Alabama, I never heard from him again. I thought that I would never love again.

Some of our friends did not make it back. Pansy's brother was a tail gunner who was Missing in Action and never returned. Those were common words. Prisoner of War was also common. We really lived in dread.

Our Own POW Camp. In Blytheville, we had a prisoner of war camp, even though the war was overseas. I often wondered why they would send prisoners to the U.S. They sometimes were used in the field for chopping cotton. It cost to use them, as labor was in demand. Once

Bud had a group of prisoners working in his field. Betty and I had reason to go talk to Bud, who was in the field with the prisoners. They had regular MPs with them too. I found out they were just like our guys...just forced to go fight. We did not mess around there too long, but long enough for one of the prisoners to show me a picture of his young son. It helped me understand more about war. Most of these guys were German. I later learned that Japanese farmers, U.S. citizens who lived here, and who we had depended on so much, were put in internment camps until after the war.

Catherine

It was after the war. Everyone but me seemed to have a purpose in life. Pauline had gone to beauty school and had opened a shop in our town. She was a very talented operator and had a thriving business. She and Bob were happily married and had a little boy by then. She was the one we turned to if we needed comfort or help – that being part of her purpose. She was always there for us – but especially for Mike and Billy.

Maryan Ruth had married Eddie Walker. My very best girlfriend, Eula Jones, had become engaged to the neighbor who grew up just down the road from us. The two people that I always ran around with were involved with their own guys. Harold Minyard and Eula were married. All these attached couples had me feeling alone and lonely. I was dating a friend, but I was only dating, not in love. I had decided love did not exist for me anymore.

Out of boredom, my friend and I would go over to the apartment where our married friends lived at that time. We were all the closest of friends. Sometimes it would be after their bedtime. We would knock on their door, get them up and say, "Come go with us – we're going to get married. So they would get out of bed and get dressed. Then we would say we changed our minds. After a few times of this, they put us to the test. The next time we knocked, they were dressed and said, "Let's go." Just like that, we went to the Justice of the Peace and got married.

Impulsive though it was, I was married and planned to make it work. But other factors were involved, and it did not work. It left me sad, restless, feeling worthless and disgusted with myself. So for the remainder of my single life, I felt out of place, not knowing what I wanted. I also knew that I had done a very stupid thing.

Mama insisted that I do something with my life. There were limited areas to excel in, in our little town, so she suggested business school. So I went to Draughon's Business School in Memphis. Boring, so boring; I needed more action. I then switched to beauty school. I graduated and became a licensed operator. Pansy went to beauty school too. I should have gone to flying school, or at least something more active and exciting. Maybe even car racing. Maybe even crop dusting – that always looked exciting to me. But by then, there was no airplane and no Harley. No boyfriend that I liked. Just plain boredom. I actually bought and managed my own beauty shop in Leachville for about a year, but that proved unsatisfying as well. Later I went back to work for Pauline, as I liked being around family and friends.

The Beauty Shop

Pauline was working in her beauty shop, which was across the street from Freeman's Mercantile in Dell. There was a decorator working in the window of Freeman's when I decided to stop by to see Pauline. I was aiming for a parking spot just short of the beauty shop. It was slant parking and, as I turned into it, the master cylinder went out and the brakes didn't hold. Acting on instinct, I pulled the car sharply to the left, thus avoiding the shop's picture window. I didn't quite make it back to the street; instead, I drove down the sidewalk past the beauty shop and the post office and coasted into the gas station on the corner. I made a perfect landing in front of the first pump and told the startled attendant, "Fill 'er up, and you better check the brakes." I was told later that the decorator had to change his clothes.

To Texas and Back

Mama married a friend, Mr. Wells, that she and Papa had known in their time in Ravenden Springs. He had also lost his wife. He lived in Texas where he had raised his family. I believe he was as restless as Mama was. She moved to Texas, letting the little boys, Mike and Billy, go with Pauline and Bob. Mr. Wells was a good man and we liked him very much. He wanted Betty and I to come live with them as well, which we did and got along very well there. We stayed almost a year. We dated a few cowboys and gained a few friends. We also visited Mexico several times. We learned how to ride a horse well and attended a few rodeos. It was a different way of life for us both.

As for Mama, it is hard to teach an old dog new tricks, and she began to think about moving back home. Mr. Wells did not want to leave Texas, and Mama wanted to go home. When Mama got a notion, you might as well go with it or she would manage to do it on her own. She moved us back home. Mr. Wells said she broke his heart. I did feel for him. Later, he gave me away in marriage.

Mama really never settled down to any routine after Papa's death. She jumped from one thing to another. One day when I was driving to town, I picked up Billy who was walking back to his dad's house where he then lived. He had big tears in his eyes. I asked, "What is wrong?" He said, "I want to live at home again." I took him back to his dad's and told Mama of the encounter with Billy. It did not take her long to go into action. She went to Doc's house and said straight out, "Doc, I want my boys back." He did not argue. By this time, he had remarried, to a lady with children.

Pauline and Bob had been living in Mama's house while she was in Texas. When she returned, Pauline had to look for a new place to live. The Luckett place had become available and they bought it. It was just made for their family. It was a terrific house. It had a nice yard and plenty of room, but best of all, Papa had built it. He had put so much into it for his very first family. It meant a lot to Pauline. Pauline and Bob had two little boys by then named John Robert and James Franklin. They lived there until they moved to California.

The Grocery Store

Mama got restless again. She decided she did not want to farm anymore, so Bud took over the farm and we moved to a much smaller house in town. Mama talked Betty and I into going into the grocery business with her. Now Mama had a dominant personality. We usually went along with her, since it was just the three of us at home. Whatever Mama wanted is usually what we did. We bought a grocery store that Mama had picked out. It was not in the best part of town. All three of us were actively working in it. I am not sure we were very good at it, but I learned to add fast, as we did not have an adding machine. Even today I can just look at numbers and know the answer. We had charge accounts for the customers. When it came pay-up time, I took page after page and added them up. Math was already my best thing, so I became really efficient in totaling up accounts.

The Cafe

Virginia and Carl had a restaurant right across the street from the armory. After their meetings, some of the national guard would come in for a snack. We were at their restaurant a lot. One of the times we were visiting, a real tragedy was in progress. One of the owners of a laundry right across from the café – and a friend to Virginia and Carl – shot and killed himself. We heard the gunshot and were caught up in the excitement when the ambulance arrived to take him away. His name was Tootsie Fox; he was the ex-husband of Dale Evans, who was raised in our area. He had been drinking and gambling and lost a lot of money. As the story went, he had called Dale and wanted her back, but she was happily married to Roy Rogers by then. I feel sure she was not interested in hearing from Tootsie.

Red

First Impressions. One particular time I was in the cafe and this guy comes in. He was nice looking, red-haired and friendly. My sister Virginia said, "Hi Red." Carl said, "Hi Red." Pauline said, "Hi Red," and a few more of the family followed suit. I thought, who is this Red that everyone seems to know but me. I just looked at him and never spoke, since I did not know him. Mama had just bought me this beautiful dress with a fur-trimmed jacket. I knew it looked good on me. Later I heard his view of our first encounter. He had never seen me before, either. His thought was: she is really into herself. She must be stuck up. It took a few times of meeting at the restaurant to begin to be friends. I found out his name was Thomas Henson.

I would tell Pauline at work, "He likes me, I can tell, but he does not ask me out." We would meet at the café to spend time with each other. After awhile, he asked to take me home. I accepted. We lived ten miles away in Dell at the time. I thought all the way home: Now this is not a date. What do I do when we get there? Just say thanks and get out, or what? I puzzled over it until we rolled up in front of the house. I kind of looked at him and reached for the door at the same time. He looked at me and put his arm around me and sort of pulled me away from the door.

That was it. I was happy to be there. He was my true love, even though we were not the least bit alike. We dated at least two or three times a week. I think I depended more on him than I ever had on anyone before. Our love was not the giddy stuff that I experienced when I was younger. It was that good old reliable feeling you have with the person you are sure about.

Fitting Together. Tom, who was a service manager in a Chevrolet agency, was well liked and had many friends. Though I had always dreamed of being married to a tall dark handsome man, my true love was a few inches shorter than me and was not dark-headed at all; he was a short handsome redhead. He was so kind and obliging to me and he took my heart away. He spoiled me and it felt good. I had always been such an independent person, thinking I had to do everything for myself. I always felt so tall with him until years later – after seeing Jackie with Onassis – when I realized that we fit together very well.

On one of our dates we went to the movies. When we came out, the ground was completely covered in snow. It was so beautiful and romantic. It felt as if the rest of the world was shut out. Just the two of us in a zone of our own. As we drove to my home, I began to wonder, how do I get in without destroying my new suede shoes. When we reached the driveway, Tom came around and opened my door, reached in, gathered me in his strong arms and carried me to my front door. He kissed me goodnight and I went in to dream. I thought I was too big to be carried. He gave me something I never had...the feeling of being little, dainty and delicate like a fairy princess being carried through the snow. He did not know the effect he had on me. I found out later he did not think I was tall – he thought he was short!

The Wedding. We dated almost a year and he was getting more amorous every time he kissed me. One night I asked myself, what is this leading to? I believed that intimacy was for married people, not singles. So just out of the blue, I said, "Let's get married." His reply, "Ok, when?" Our wedding date was set right there and then. There was one requirement: I would not marry him without a proposal. He proposed. Then I planned the wedding that I wanted. Our wedding date was set for three months off. Tom would have liked to have a big church wedding. He had lots of friends; his work put him in direct contact with the public. However, I wanted a wedding at home with mostly family members.

There was a lot to do: clothes to be bought, flowers to be picked out. We had to decide where in the house to put an altar, among other things.

During this preparation stage, one of our customers sent word that he was sick, and he asked if one of the bosses would come see him. Well, Mom sent me. He was a very nice black man that had traded with us faithfully. He needed surgery urgently but could not pay for it. He needed $80 just to get admitted to the hospital. I told him I would ask Mama. When I did, I told her that he could have the money that was set aside for my wedding dress, if need be. Mama sent him the money. He had his surgery and soon got well enough to go back to work. Did we get the money back? No, but we did what was important.

Betty and I were going to Memphis to shop for wedding clothes. And yes, Mama made sure I had money for my wedding dress. Our bus got into Memphis very early in the morning, so we window-shopped for a while. We had most things picked out before the stores opened. It was a fun day for us. We had our attire in hand, including Betty's dress, by time to go home. Betty was my maid of honor.

Everything was ready for the wedding. We had candle arbors across one corner of the room with an altar behind. We marched in to 'Clair de Lune.' Even now when I hear that song it touches me very much. We were married April 20, 1947.

After the Wedding. Now you have to know how nervous we both were; when he pronounced us man and wife, I kissed him and smelt booze on his breath. *That's* why he had been sneaking over to our new home next door; he was trying to cure his nervousness. When everyone came around to offer congratulations, each of my sisters just walked by me and gave Tom a big lipstick kiss. So not only was he smelling of whiskey, he had lipstick all over his face. We got off to a slightly rocky start. When it was time to leave for the honeymoon, we took off in a car with tin cans tied to it, as well as bottles and ribbons and any other tacky thing possible. We got three blocks away, both of us so wanting to be anywhere else. I asked him to stop and get rid of the mess on the car. He was beside himself and kept going. We had our first quarrel before we got out of town. I could not stand to be so public and sort of went to pieces, so he stopped and got rid of the cans on the car. We continued on our way and pretty soon we both started settling down. In the end, we had a lovely honeymoon.

I loved my in-laws. Tom's mother, Lilly, was the most giving, gracious person. She always treated me like I was special. She had taken care of an older couple while she raised her own family. I know it had to be hard on her husband Louis. He had to keep both places up. They had made her the beneficiary to their property. She continued caring for them the rest of their lives.

Tom

Tom was not a person to speak out in a hurry; he thought things over before speaking. I never heard him talk bad about anyone. He was not the least judgmental.

Settling In. My sister Vida had a house right next door to Mama in Blytheville. Vida and her husband were in Texas. We rented their house and moved in right after our honeymoon. If I had it to do all over

86

again, I would have moved across town. We were just a little too convenient to everyone. When Mama came to my back door and called my name, I thought I had to jump and see what she wanted.

When we went out to see his folks who lived in the country, Betty and Mary, my sister Johnnie's daughter, would come in and take over, getting into whatever pleased them. My new husband could have been annoyed, but he never complained about such little inconveniences. He liked all of my family and enjoyed people, in general. Thank goodness for that, because I was among the people that I loved the most.

We had built a small house on the back of Mama's lot. For our protection, she had the lot put in Betty's and my names. Mama had a large lot, so there was plenty of room for two houses.

Anniversary Present. Ten days before our first anniversary, Kathryn Ann was born. When I came home from the hospital – to my surprise – Tom had put new venetian blinds on all our windows. In our day, that was a big thing. Our new baby was here, our house was decorated, and Tom had a boss that really liked him and gave him the whole week off to take care of me and the new baby. We had many reasons to be happy.

I understand why my sister Vida thought Tom was a hero. He came to her rescue several times in her young life. One of those times, when her son was so sick with pneumonia, he was the one with her in the hospital. I should have been up there helping Vida; instead it was my husband. He would go over on his lunch break and give Vida a chance to go get something to eat. After work, he would go to hospital again and sit with Jimmy while Vida got out a little bit. I guess I was so involved with my own interests that I did not even realize that I was negligent.

I was living in sheer bliss and starting to want another baby. Ann was three months old then. A couple of months later, I got pregnant, and then I thought, *why did I do this?*

Some Changes

Mama decided she wanted out of the grocery store, so she did some maneuvering. She put the store in our names, mine and Tom's, and had us put our half interest in the lot (which included the house) into Betty's name. She took off, free and clear, back to her house on the farm, where she always wanted to be anyway.

We managed our own life after that, as did Betty. Betty married soon after Mama left. We were all friends and spent a lot of time together. She also started her family; her first was Fredrick Jo. Betty and Gaston Taylor, her husband, moved to Michigan. Looking back, I wish they had stayed closer to me.

Bang, Bang, Daddy

We had living quarters in the back of the grocery store, and that is where Carolyn Faye was born, in June of 1948. By this time, Tom was working full time in the store. One night we had not yet closed when a big, strong-looking black man came into the store. He began to make me a little uneasy by the way he was acting. He managed to steer Tom to the meat counter, which was away from the checkout counter. The checkout counter was a little cubbyhole. I was feeling pretty nervous about his presence, so I reached down and pulled out a small gun we kept for emergencies, tripped the safety, and laid it close at hand. Tom had also become uneasy. As he was showing him the meat (that we suspected he did not really want), Tom was waving a three-foot-long meat cleaver and talking to him at the same time. We both felt we were about to be robbed. For some reason – *the meat cleaver maybe?* – the guy left and we closed up. The next day we were standing in this same cubbyhole when Ann, who was maybe two, was standing at our feet. I looked down just in time to see her with the pistol in her hands saying, "Bang, bang, Daddy." It was cocked, so that her little finger could have easily pulled the trigger. We both went a little white. He secured the gun that I had carelessly left out. I do not think I ever pulled it out again.

In Memphis with Elvis

In time, we left the grocery store; it was not what we wanted to do anyway. We sold it and Tom went to work in Memphis at Hart's Bakery. He was in charge of their fleet of delivery trucks. I went to work in a beauty shop. At that time, Elvis Presley worked as a delivery man for the same bakery as Tom. He had his own little band. At night, he and his guys would get together and practice. Little did we know how famous he would become. We were there about a year.

Elvis became richer and we became poorer. We were just not satisfied in Memphis. One day Tom came home and stated, "We are going to California." That suited me to a T. So we all went to California – Elvis to Hollywood, us to Torrance. The two decisions were not connected. It just happened that way.

California – A Great Move

Getting a Start. Back then, you could pay a deposit on a rental car, drive it through to its destination, and get your deposit back when you turned the car in. So it only cost us for gas and lodging. Virginia and Carl were in California, so we stayed with them as long as Carl could stand it. It might have been two weeks.

Virginia and Carl had a wonderful daughter that helped occupy our girls. She was very good with them. Carl took Tom to apply for a job on the assembly line at General Motors. He got the job, but when he came out, Carl was gone. He had provided one-way transportation only. Tom caught a bus and walked a few miles, eventually finding his way back home.

Tom had a job, but no car. His work was about 25 miles away. I do not remember any lack of confidence on his part about overcoming these obstacles. Determined, he started going through used car lots until he found a means of transportation. He ran into a guy by the name of J.W. Simpson from our town of Blytheville. Tom told him what he needed and J.W. found a car for him. He was able to arrange a delayed down payment, which would allow him time to get his first paycheck. Carl helped him rent a two-room apartment in a little motel and introduced him to a grocery store that took credit. I knew that Heavenly Father was looking out for us.

We were not without a church home for long. Before we made the trip to California, we had discussed finding a church and transferring our membership there. The very first thing we did was find a Baptist church to attend. I had been raised Methodist, but Tom was Baptist. For the next few years, we took ourselves and our kids to the Keystone Baptist Church.

Not long after our move, my sister Betty and her husband Gaston also moved to California. Then later Pauline and Bob. Carl and Virginia, of course, were already there. Our children were very close to each other. We had lots of good times together. Betty lived close to me and she watched my kids while I worked. She was always there for me when I needed her.

Betty and her family lived in California until her daughter Kay was about five years old. Then they moved to Kentucky – a world away from us – to my sorrow.

Tom made a move to McDonnell Douglas Aircraft and became a tool and die maker. To further his career in the aircraft business, he attended El Camino College in Redondo Beach and gained two years of college education. Had we not been living in California, he would not have had this opportunity. Tom remained in the aircraft business as long as he worked in California. He had always been ambitious. In Arkansas, Tom had gone to work before he got out of high school, and went straight into management at the end of his last school year.

California was a great move for us. At that particular time, lots of people from other states were migrating to California, finding opportunities there not available in other places. I began to realize this was a worker's paradise.

One of many things that amazed me about California was: when you went to the bank, you would see people in boots, work clothes, and every possible kind of dress. At home, we always dressed proper when we went to the bank.

Moving Around. I went into sales. I did Stanley Home Products for a few years, then changed to Fashion Two Twenty, a cosmetic line. I went from a shy country girl to an aggressive salesperson. My whole world began to blossom out. It was a good time in my life. We were always busy doing something fun. We went to the desert a lot, took our kids horseback riding, and joined a recreation camp with lots of family activities.

When Ann was 13, we lived in Torrance and I was still in sales. She had become a regular teenager, wanting to think for herself. Unfortunately, she took up with a group of teens that we did not approve of at all, and we became alarmed for her future. An opportunity came up to move to Huntington Park. That was a good move, for Ann especially. It put her right in the middle of some good kids that belonged to the Mormon church. She went with them to Mutual, a church program for kids. She really liked the bishop's son, who went on his mission when he became old enough. Faye was very involved with the Baptist church. She attended a Billy Graham revival and also sang in the choir, along with Dale Evans and Roy Rogers, among others.

Eventually, we moved back to Torrance and bought a house there. Pauline's family and mine spent many hours together. Tacos on Saturday night was a big thing for us. Bobby, Frankie, Ann and Faye were very close to each other and did many fun things as a group. We got together and told stories of the past, which kept us laughing. Our favorite place was the beach. A trip to the beach was almost a daily occurrence as the kids were growing up. My car almost always had sand in it.

Virginia and Carl had moved to New Mexico and opened a pawn shop in Alamogordo. We would stop and visit them on our way to Arkansas for vacations. We went back every year to see our folks.

I took a job at a place called Ace Bag Lunch. I was driving a lunch truck delivering lunches to longshoremen, and other places along the way. I drove the lunch truck on Terminal Island for oil workers. It made me a little nervous, because the island would tremble from all the oil rigs there. This was right on the great Pacific Ocean. Once when I was driving the lunch truck, we had so much rain – a rarity in California – that I could not get home to pick up my kids until the water drained down.

After a while, I tried my hand at a factory, but I had to overcome a fear of big machinery. I don't know why, but that was my phobia. My girlfriend had gotten me a job there. Due to our circumstances, I needed this job. I went in the first morning and was shown this big break machine that cut out certain parts of a door. I had to put a long strip of wood into the machine for it to cut out the parts. I held the strip of wood in the machine that came down over my hands, thinking I have to do this even if it cuts my hands off. The breaks went down, with a big shush sound, over my hands and came up again; I was amazed that I still had hands. One good thing about the factory, it put an end to my phobia about machinery.

Tom in the Kitchen

Tom was helpful with many things, but I learned to be cautious when asking for his help in the kitchen. Once, I had to be gone for a few days, visiting my sister Virginia in New Mexico. When it was time for dinner, as told to me by my girls, he decided to have pork chops. He heated the skillet – probably way too high – and put the pork chops on to cook. Grease shot out at him and burned him. Being a redhead and quick to temper, he threw the fork he was turning the meat with into the sink. It bounced back and hit him in the head. This upset him even more, so he opened the silverware drawer for another fork with such force that the whole drawer went in the floor. At this point in the story, the girls and I were hysterical with laughter. The story ended with them trying to eat the crispy pork chops. They just went crunch, crunch but they didn't dare say a word; they just ate them.

They told me this story one night when we were spending the night together. We laughed so hard, there was no sleep in sight for a while.

The Test Pilot

As time traveled on, our children began to choose careers of their own. Gene Mooney, brother Bud's son, having been brought up in the back seat of a plane, chose flying. He became a test pilot for the Air Force. He was the same little boy who said to his dad during a forced landing, "Are you going to make it, Dad?" It is evident that Gene grew up with a desire to fly. He went bigger and higher, into the cockpit of a jet. He had joined the Air Force at an early age and spent 25 years serving our country. His dad lived out in the country about ten miles from the nearest airbase. When Gene chose to visit him, he would fly over his house and buzz him a few times. That was the signal for Bud to go pick him up. Bud would drive out to the base, and they would visit overnight. Then his dad would take him back to the base and he would fly on to his destination.

Gene flew at least 83 missions over Vietnam during the war. He received the Meritorious Service Medal, the Distinguished Flying Cross and seven other flying medals. He retired as a high ranking officer and went on to do some work for NASA. I do know his Dad was proud of him.

Donna

My sister Vida and her family lived in Forrest City, Arkansas. Their daughter Donna, who had married and divorced, had custody of her little boy Eddie. They were living with Vida and Haywood. Eddie made life wonderful for his grandparents.

One day, Donna had gone to the store and had little two-year old Eddie with her. They were walking home when her ex drove up beside her in his truck and got out with a gun in his hand. He gave Donna a big shove and put Eddie in the truck, all the time holding the gun on Donna. He drove off with Eddie, leaving Donna crying and distraught. He then disappeared off the face of the earth. No one could find him. Five years went by. They searched everywhere they knew, but found nothing on the whereabouts of the ex or the boy. Haywood spent every spare dime he had to search for that baby.

Each year on our vacation, we went by to visit them. They were still in despair and grieving. One summer, as we were again discussing

Eddie's disappearance, Tom thoughtfully suggested they try searching in California. In those years, that was a good place to disappear in. It turned out to be a good suggestion; the first time Haywood sent out an enquiry, he came up with an address in Redondo Beach, California. It was just ten miles away from where we lived. The ex-husband had used his real name for a security clearance for a job. Considering five years had passed, he must have felt safe. Haywood had traced him through his social security number.

This is where the tension got hot and heavy; we were all involved. Haywood put Donna on the plane to us with a letter to the lawyer that Tom had secured to represent Donna. The letter explained the situation and what he knew.

My teenagers and their friend Linda went to work on it too. The girls tried a stakeout at the address that they had, but there was no evidence of anyone being there. Linda called the school where they would be going if they lived at that address. She posed as a social services worker and left our number to call back. Wow! We could have been in so much trouble. She did get a call back with information that the kids were registered in a school in Orange County. We got an address for the school.

Since Donna still had legal custody of Eddie, the lawyer told her if she saw Eddie, to just take off with him. At our house, everyone was on edge. We were all so involved in the rescue of this one little boy. Donna went to the school to watch for Eddie when the school was dismissed for the day. She was so intent, watching, waiting and hoping to see her son. As the school let out, she saw a familiar child, but five years had passed, and she could not be sure. Doubting herself, she did not approach him.

The lawyer had involved the Orange County police in the case, and they were waiting on Donna when we arrived at the police station.

They went to the address that was registered to her ex-husband and asked for him. The woman who answered the door said he was not there. The police kept us informed of each event as it occurred, but they didn't tell us they had staked out every exit from his house. We were sitting in that police station fit to be tied. The policemen were pretty tense too.

Within a few minutes, he left his house with Eddie and got in his truck, planning to disappear again. When he got to the corner, he was stopped. They took him and Eddie, and relieved him of the gun he was carrying. The excitement did not stop there. They took him to jail and Eddie to the police station where we were waiting. They called us into an interior office for Donna and Eddie to reunite. They asked Eddie, "Do you know this woman?" Eddie answered, "No." Then they said to Donna, "Do you know this child?" and she said, "No."

Donna just stood there in disbelief, not recognizing the child who had grown up so much in the years he had been gone. From age two to seven. Wow, wow. I held my breath and so did all the policemen in the room. Donna was crying by then, and the little boy was so scared. The suspense was overwhelming. I know the officers were thinking the same as I was: they had the wrong child.

After a long silence, the little boy started talking about other kids and mentioning their names. One officer asked, "Do you know who he is talking about?" Donna replied, "His brothers." You could feel the tension leave the room and relief began to take its place. But Donna was still quiet, just listening.

Eddie continued to talk. To his mother he said, "Are you my dumb Donna?" His mind had been poisoned against Donna. At this point, I began to talk to Eddie. I assured him this was his mother and she had missed him so much and loved him so much and had tried to find him for so long. Then I asked him, "Would you like to give your mother a big hug?" He nodded his head and they embraced. We, including the officers, were happy to see justice being achieved.

When he was released, we put him and Donna in the back seat of the car, and they both giggled all the way home. On the attorney's advice, we put them both on a plane back to Arkansas. The dad never contacted him again.

The Post Office

After trying a few other jobs, I decided to try out for postal employee. I passed the test and worked for the post office for 13 years. The postal world was unlike any other. It was as if the rest of the world did not exist. We ate, slept and breathed the operation of mail. I started out as an indefinite temp, which meant I did a little bit of everything. I carried special delivery mail. I picked up mail from mail drops. I worked on the line sorting mail. I went from station to station to work. It was an interesting job and I loved it. We had to memorize all the streets of each carrier's route to know where to put the mail. We had to know every zip code in order to to punch the right keys for mail out of town. Not only that, but we were subject to mandatory overtime when it was needed. We worked 12 hours a day, 7 days a week at Christmas time.

However, the best part for me – everyone was my friend. We lived, laughed and enjoyed our work.

My lifestyle had changed, but not all for the better. The very thing I feared the most when we came to California – getting too much into social drinking – was exactly what I did. When I came home from a 12-hour day, I would have a glass of wine to relax me. Every time some one retired from the post office, we would have a party at some big center and have food, drinks, and a lot of dancing. I fast became the life of the party. It was too much. This went on for a few years. My girls grew into teenagers. I had been very strict in training them, but now my own life was getting out of whack. I was not living the life I really believed in.

Helping Betty

Betty's marriage had met a disastrous end. It was now just Betty and the children. You just have to know how close we all were and how well we understood each other. My girls really loved her children and hers mine. Fred came to live with us the year before Betty came to California. When Fred called to say he was at the bus station in LA, I could not go because of work so I sent the girls. When they arrived at the bus station, Ann tapped Fred on the shoulder to let him know they were there, and he came around ready to swing at her. He had already had an encounter with a gay guy. What a relief to see his cousins. They bonded very fast and always had time for each other. Over the years, they have held onto that feeling. Even now, they consider him the only brother they ever had. When Betty and the rest of her family moved back to California, they stayed with us for a short time before she got her own place.

I can be really proud of Tom; he looked out for us all. He spent many hours with Betty's son Timmy. He took him to get his haircuts, even though Tim would get mad because he always had to get a butch cut. That was his pet peeve; however, I do not think he ever complained to Tom about it. Tom's delight was buying new shoes or boots for Tim. He had never dealt with boys before Fred and Tim. I have to say that Fred was a handful when he got there, but it did not stop us from loving him dearly.

Fred went to work in a retail store – though he was not really old enough – a place called Lenard's. We had to drive him there and back. Tom was the one who looked out for him, as I was super-involved with the postal express.

Missionaries

Something to Live For. Faye had dropped out of teenage social life. She was not into parties and was not enjoying this phase of growing up. Her friends would ask where Faye was and why she didn't attend their events. In fact, they started calling her Sister Faye, maybe because she seemed nun-like and religious to them. I have to say, neither of my girls ever got into real trouble. The thing I tried to impress upon them most was that if drugs came in one door, they go out the other. That advice worked for them.

One day, Faye told me she had prayed for Heavenly Father to send her something to live for. Heavenly Father heard her prayer; two Mormon missionaries knocked on our door. Ann answered it. They left her a Book of Mormon and made an appointment to come back and see her the next day. It just happened in those days that Ann was always busy with friends and did not – in her mind – have time to stay home and wait for missionaries. Standing them up offended Faye's sense of fairness, so she made an effort to be there when they arrived. We all benefited from Faye's decision.

Our whole life began to change. The missionaries began to give Faye lessons. I shall always be thankful for a young missionary named Brunel Hyde Hall and his companion. It was not long until Faye was baptized into the Church of Jesus Christ of Latter Day Saints. The rest of us were beginning to get involved also, but I had more to overcome. I smoked, drank coffee and had an occasional cocktail. I will never forget the terrible time I had going through withdrawal from cigarettes. The missionaries made numerous trips by the house each day while I was stressing. Each trip, they would bring me something, like a candy bar, to help me. Toward the end of the first day, they brought me a cigarette holder and told me to suck on that, which I did. Their help made all the difference.

I apologized to my friends at the post office for being so snappy and asked them to forgive me because I was quitting cigarettes. Everyone there knew what was going on, as we were a close-knit group. I gave up the cigarettes, and Ann and I were baptized at the same time.

We all became missionaries. I sent missionaries to everyone that would listen, including my friends at the post office. We had as many people as would come, to our house for discussions. In fact, we had 22 'first discussions' in our living room. We had dinners and invited the missionaries and lots of other people. Just to be clear, our growing church involvement took place over a span of years that overlap with stories of other important life events, like marriages and births.

At one of the dinners after I became a grandma, I had made Cornish hens; they made a beautiful array of food with all the other things I had. We started passing the food round and each took a gorgeous, ornate Cornish hen. When it came time for my granddaughter Cindy to have her plate fixed – she was maybe two by then – she looked at the Cornish hens with big tears in her eyes and started saying, "Poor chicky, poor chicky." To the rest of us, the food tasted good, but I think everyone felt guilty eating those chickens.

Betty and her family joined us in having the missionaries over. All her family was baptized, as well, except for Tim, who was just six. He was often heard saying "and just why can't I be baptized?" We kept telling him he would have to wait until he was eight...but he was not convinced.

Faye had twin girlfriends, Brenda and Sandy, who were in dire straits. The girls attended high school with Faye and had become fast friends. They had been put in the care of an aunt, who evidently was only interested in what she was being paid by the state. Their mother had died and left several children. The father could not handle all the responsibilities that were left to him. The aunt had made it clear that when the girls turned 18, they were 'out of there.' They joined our group of investigators (people who were exploring the Mormon faith). They were baptized into the church and Heavenly Father helped them find their way. They both got jobs at 18 and, in time, they both married and started their own families.

Problems to Resolve. There was one big negative for me – Tom supported our church activities, but did not participate himself. He was not at my side. He did attend several priesthood seminars with me and he did some wonderful things for us. When he learned we needed food storage, he took us out to a food staging place and bought us $1,000-worth of hermetically packed food that was guaranteed for 15 years. Plus a wheat grinder and a bread maker. He even talked food storage at work to some inactive members. But he stood fast in his position not to join the church; we could not move him to be baptized. He was for us all the way, but he still visited the bar for a few drinks from time to time. His refusal did do a job on me.

We kind of went in different directions. I had always depended on him so much, and this was a whole different ballgame. Three separate times, it got the best of me and I gave in. Each time, I would go hunting for him and find him at the bar. The fact that I joined him was the very worst thing for me. I was a tormented soul. I thought a lot about it and I prayed about it also. I came to one firm conclusion – he would have to join me; I could not and would not join him. My words to him, "I cannot serve two masters. You can go to the bar if you choose. You can go your own way, but I am doing what I know I have to do. I am living the gospel, and I am going to church."

When I made that strong decision, I felt that I might be giving up my marriage, but I stood firm. It was the only way for me. Like magic – or a miracle – that was the last time Tom went to the bar. That does not mean he joined me in church, or left off his coffee or cigarettes, but now there was hope along with frustration.

There was another problem that was more easily resolved. The position that I held at work required me to work on Sundays, which kept me from attending church. Eventually, I was able to bid on another job and have Sundays off; I was finally able to attend church regularly.

Faye had problems too. She went to Palmyra, New York to participate in the church pageant that is held there every year. She met a girlfriend in Salt Lake and they traveled together and both were in the pageant. When she returned to Utah, she was sick – even then she had a thyroid condition – and her car was not working. Her dad got on a plane carrying his toolbox (*can you imagine that today?*). He arrived in Salt Lake with tools in hand, ready to work on her car. He fixed her car and drove her home. As they passed the Salt Lake temple, he surprised Faye with a request to go through the missionary center; it was a good omen, which of course made Faye happy.

Betty in Osceola

Betty, Carol and Timmy moved back to Osceola, Arkansas close to Mary Lee. Kay married Fui Tusiesiena. Fred married Elaine. Soon after they arrived in Osceola, Carol went to work. There was no local church; the closest one was in Hayti, Missouri. However, that did not dampen their church spirit. Carol discovered that the bread delivery man was a member of the Mormon church, and they were able to get together with him for family home evenings. A few years later, Carol went away to college in Jonesboro. Lo and behold, there was an LDS church. I know she must have felt like she had come home.

None of my other family members or Tom's became involved with the church. Just Betty's family and mine. Even so, that small core group spread the word to a lot of people. This included, for example, the people that had attended discussions in our home, and friends of our children who were introduced to the church through them.

New Directions

Ann went to Hawaii to marry Johnny Miller who was in the Army and stationed there. Tom and I joined her in Hawaii for the wedding, and then followed that up with a great vacation. Their daughter Cindy was born there in October of 1970.

Faye was single, but dating a guy who was getting ready for his mission. She was very active in church affairs. In fact, when I answered the phone, I felt like saying "Faye's residence." Things had changed drastically for her. From refusing practically any contact with other young people, she had completely blossomed out. The future was looking good, except I still had that nagging feeling of incompleteness without Tom at my side.

We moved into a new ward and I was a primary worker. There was a single man in this ward who also worked in primary. How I got put on the singles list I do not know, but it happened. I knew he was watching me and would consider making friends. I managed to stay out of his way because I did not want to embarrass him. I did mention it to Tom, which had no effect on him one way or the other. It surely did not motivate him to go with me.

One time the guy followed me part of the way home. I did not know how to handle it other than going straight up to him and saying I am married. Thankfully, the situation took care of itself. We had not had home teachers call on us yet, as I was pretty new in the ward. One knock on the door solved the matter: there were our home teachers, and this same guy was one of them. After they left, I told my husband he was the one that thought I was single. Tom said, "Is that why you almost fell off your chair?" with a grin on his face. It was kind of funny, but also embarrassing not knowing how to handle the situation. I had just avoided him rather than dealing with it.

Wallace

Mama's stepdad, Wallace Perry, was growing older. His funds were limited and Mama was aware of it. She took the very back bedroom of her house, the one built for the little boys when they came to live with us, and made it into a bedroom for Wallace. He lived there until he died. Mama had a saying, "There is always room for one more" and she lived by that rule. I grew up believing that also.

Mr. Bob

Mama married again, to a friend of many years. Bob Minyard and his family had lived on our land until after Papa died and then he bought his own acreage. His wife, Lula, had helped Mama weekly with her many chores, particularly washing and ironing. Mr. Bob was a big help in many ways, but he was especially valuable during hog killing time.

He was a fine man and a good friend to Papa. He was there for Papa when he died. He sat in the vigil with several other men, in the room where Papa lay until his funeral.

When they married, it was the first time I had seen Mama happy and settled since Papa's death. He was the only Grandpa Betty's kids knew and they loved him. They lived very close to Mama and Mr. Bob.

Our (Intended) Retirement Home in Missouri

Tom, Faye and I made a trip to Missouri to buy a home for our retirement. Up front, we decided we would only buy a house where there was a church. We found and bought a beautiful country home with ten acres in West Plains that we liked very much. Faye, being restless, decided she wanted to move to Missouri right then. She talked her granddad into staying with her. She and her dad's father occupied the house contentedly for a while.

While there, she was introduced to a young guy from California. His Name was Larry Campbell. He also had land in West Plains and happened to be visiting the area. He was going to school at Cal Poly in California, majoring in agriculture. His school was not too far from where we lived, and he knew some of the same people that we knew in California.

Tom and I were getting ready for retirement even though it was not yet time. Tom had never liked being locked up in any form or fashion. When he went in to work at McDonnell Douglas, the gates were always locked with a guard on duty. It made him feel trapped. The next best thing to freedom for him was planning for our retirement. I had already moved furniture into our country place, which – as it turned out – may have been rushing things a bit.

I think maybe some of the decisions I made created the excitement in our marriage. Tom sure let me have my freedom whenever I chose to do something. He told my sister Pauline that living with me was like being on the tail end of a kite. The Missouri house was a case in point: we had a fully furnished house in Missouri for a retirement that was off in the future, and only a few leftover pieces of furniture in our California apartment where we actually lived. I was my mother's daughter, needless to say. Our future home in Missouri turned out to be – if not a retirement home – a nice vacation spot for us.

Faye and Larry

A Temple Wedding. Faye came back to California from Missouri and soon became reacquainted with the guy she had met in Missouri. They started dating and eventually were married in the Los Angeles Temple. I could not get a temple recommend (which has to do with worthiness and meeting church requirements), because back then, unless your spouse was also a member, you could not have one. Therefore, I could not go to Faye's wedding. That was a hard thing to explain to my non-member friends. I did accept it, though...with a small ache in my heart.

Their First Home. Plans have a way of getting changed. Faye and Larry started their new life in our fully furnished house in West Plains, Missouri. Larry had land there also and was familiar with that part of the country. Not long afterward they started their family, giving me plenty of reasons to visit her and the rest of my family not far away in Arkansas. Betty and her family spent time visiting there also.

Faye became pregnant with Matthieu and became very ill with toxemia, which lasted all through her pregnancy. I managed to be there for the baby's arrival, but it was a touch-and-go situation whether she would make it or not. It was on a Monday night – I remember because the whole ward was asked to pray for her. She and Matt pulled through, but it was still iffy for a few days for both. Matthieu Thomas Campbell was born in January of 1975.

They were back in California by the time Daniel was born in 1976. After another year, they moved back to Missouri to Larry's farm, where Joshua was born. Their house did not have indoor plumbing but had the water in, so it could be converted. Tom became duly alarmed – a new baby with no plumbing and only an outdoor toilet. Tom went out there for several days to help. They hired a guy in their ward that installed bathrooms, but he was not making theirs a priority. He would work a while and then leave. One night, Tom heard Faye crying because she needed a shower. Larry took her to the back porch and helped her get a shower from the hose. The next day when the plumber showed up, Tom laid down the law: he could not go home until that bath was put in. He finished the bath, and I felt kind of bad for the guy. I think he realized that if he had dared leave, he would have heard about it.

Even though we had bought another house in California by then – *and* had it completely furnished – I still spent as much time in Missouri as I could. The church there started out in an old building with not many members, but over time the branch became a ward with a new building. Faye and Larry spent time in both Missouri and California, working some and going to school. Their family continued to grow. They finally purchased their own house in West Plains after selling their land, and Larry finished his education at Columbia, Missouri. He became an extension agent for the University.

The next baby for Faye and Larry was Carolina Rose, born in June of 1986. They were living close to me at that time; I was in Arkansas, but not far from West Plains, Missouri.

I loved to take Carolina home with me. When she was about two, she would be sleeping in her crib, and I would say, "Carolina, do you want to go with me?" Even before she could get awake, she would raise her little leg like she was trying to get up and then struggle to open her eyes. Then she was ready to go. Carolina and I both had the same go-power, I think.

Vida

I made trips to Vida trying to interest her in the gospel. She was always in tune with what seemed right at the moment. She said we made a Mormon out of her every day, and Haywood made a Baptist out of her every night. Vida Ray died in 1972, a few months before Mama. We did her temple work as soon as possible. Though she hadn't converted, there was strong evidence of her acceptance of the Mormon faith.

Mama's Death

When my mother became ill, I spent as much time with her as possible. On one of my trips there, I decided to reach out to one of her sisters-in-law for information about Mama's side of the family to add to my genealogy. My mother's bed was in the same room as the telephone. My sister Virginia was taking care of her at the time. I had already gotten all the information from Mom that she had. As I was talking to Cordie, her brother Pull Ray's wife, Mama was listening. She was in and out on memory by then. She kept hearing me ask questions about her family and tried to answer from her bed. She kept saying, "My mother's name was Anna Eddings." She kept repeating the same thing. I could hear her, but I needed to get Cordie's information, so I was kind of ignoring what Mom was saying. Finally, when she couldn't get my attention, Mama said to Virginia, "Will you tell that tall loudmouth blond from California to shut up." That left us all with a sweet sense of her good humor, because Mom was still partly in tune with us. Not long afterwards, my mother died, on February 20, 1973. She was 86 years old.

Mama was a dynamic person. She had married a 41-year old man, had 13 children and raised four more. To the end of her days, she had the regard and loyalty of all her kids. She reigned like a queen and we all loved her.

Our Latest New Retirement Home

As we were getting closer to retirement, we took a vacation and went looking for another property, since we had sold the house in West Plains. There were two things I did not have much say-so in, one in real estate and the other in cars. Tom found the house he liked on ten acres and would not budge. It was not big enough to suit me and it was five miles outside the city limit sign, so that made it even farther to town. It was still under construction and, since I had no say-so in the location, I redesigned the house to suit me. A would-be two-car garage was made into a nice big den. There would be two fireplaces, one in the den and one in the living room. The 'two-car garage' would be built to my specifications, as I wanted an extra room for my own. I was taking a class in upholstery and thought I might do that after I moved; if so, I would need space for it. The room was finished with insulation, a flue for a wood stove, and windows to suit me. It ended up being a nice home. Tom built himself a garage later on.

Being a Grandma

Ann and Johnnie had parted ways. I really feel like his stint in the Vietnam War had left him a little unpredictable and not a steady husband. And he did not have the church to help steady him. Cindy had been born in Hawaii. Not only did the divorce leave Ann torn up, it shattered Cindy. She had been with her dad more than anyone else, and they were so close. Because of her demanding job, Ann could not give her the attention she was used to after the split. She had been the center of her dad's life; then to be completely ignored, by comparison, was almost too much for Cindy. Even though she was the first grandchild from Ann, and I tried spoiling her rotten, it did not always take. Although she spent lots of time at our house, it couldn't replace her dad.

Cindy had a way of getting into her granddad's drawer and eating his cough drops. He would complain when not even one was left. Therefore, I told Cindy, please do not take the last cough drop, as granddad really needs them to help him sleep. A few days later she came over again. That night when we started to bed, Tom said, "I see Cindy was over today." I immediately asked if she ate all his cough drops. "No, she left one." Well, what did he expect, that's what I asked her to do. The cough drop story would always make us laugh.

When my second grandchild Matthieu was visiting later, he saw Cindy into granddad's cough drops. She always ate the red ones first; cherry was most to her liking. They looked so good to Matt. He grabbed one and started eating it. He coughed and spit for the next hour. What is one man's treasure is another man's trash, as Papa would have said. It was the last cough drop for Matt, ever. Ever.

Like most grandmas, I loved my grandchildren, but I was somewhat over-possessive. I think I would have completely taken over had it not been for a little opposition from the parents. So, since I did not have control over my grandkids, I made up for it with the things I bought them. I had certain places that I shopped. Toys-R-Us, for instance. Clothes were another frequent shopping opportunity. Faye ended up with four boys so close together I did not have to worry about size; I could buy a two, three or four and it would fit one of them. So that is how I spent my days off. I think my daughters did not cherish me like my grandkids did.

Ann married again. Her new husband was Russell Pike. They moved to Long Beach, California. He had three children and custody of his oldest daughter, Amy. Amy loved her dad like Cindy had loved Johnny. Amy did not get close to her mother until she was grown, and Cindy never got close to her dad again. Too bad kids have to suffer for the choices grown-ups make.

We continued to make our trips to Missouri; we could not move yet as we were both still working. We just could not get ourselves with our furniture. On one of the trips to Missouri, what I had waited so long for came to pass – Tom was baptized into the church. Lilly was four days old. Her mother brought her down from Appleton City, Missouri, where Larry was county agent, for the baptizing. We had to go right back to California, so Tom never actually got involved in church activities. Not back to square one, but not all the way there.

I retired from the Post Office, but Tom would not let go of a regular paycheck, even though his health was failing. Later, he was forced to retire.

We sold our house in California and I moved our third set of furniture to Missouri. Tom stayed with Russ and Ann, and I flitted back and forth for a while. When Ann became pregnant with Scott, I stayed and helped out there. And it was a good thing I did. Her work was so demanding – she was in advertising – that her office was calling her for answers even while she was in labor. After Scott was born, I took the phone off the hook for her to nurse the baby. Russ was in law school as well as working. Scott was almost ours. His granddad spent many hours talking and playing with him. We had so much love for him. As a baby, Scott would move his little mouth and make sounds like he was talking back.

We were getting ready to move to Missouri, finally, after Tom was kicked out with a pension. Since we were leaving, Russ hired a nanny from Ireland to care for the kids. Her name was Rosemary, and we became the best of friends. She was so good with Scott. Later she married my sister Pauline's son Frank. We loved her and loved having her in the family.

Retirement – Sort of

Working Harder than Ever. After we moved to Missouri, I have to say I never worked so hard in my life. We had two big gardens. Tom's dad, who had come to stay with us, really knew how to make a garden. I canned food until I was blue in the face. My grocery bill was almost nothing, but my back and hands were paying for it. Matthieu was old enough then to pick blackberries, so I paid him two dollars a gallon and put the berries in the freezer. Matt was such a good boy and ambitious. He was so willing to help me. One day, I asked him if he would wash down my cabinets and he worked all morning on them. Then he asked to go to Walmart to spend the money he had made. He showed signs of a cold and was sneezing. Just before we left, I suggested he take a dose of Benadryl. He protested, but I gave it to him anyway. Just as I drove up to Walmart's parking lot, I looked over and Matt was snoring with his mouth open. I felt so mean. I had worked him so hard all morning that it put him to sleep. It didn't occur to me at first that it was the medicine that put him to sleep. Fortunately, he did wake up in time to go shopping.

Making Adjustments. I became restless and bored. I had not yet made the transition from city life to country living. I had left all my friends behind, and my new neighbors were not close enough to suit me. I was attending church off and on, but not enough to keep me involved, as I should have been. Rather than go to church, Tom got up every Sunday morning, took his bath, put on his better clothes and got in front of the TV to watch some kind of preaching. I pleaded with him for city life again; he offered to move to Springfield. That shut me up in a hurry because I did not like Springfield as a residence. Faye and Larry had moved to Utah. Tom was not much on trips, so I would have been stuck in the country, were it not for Betty. Her daughter Carol was also in Utah, so Betty and I took trips together to see our kids. Tom was always happy to be left behind. It seems plain that he liked the house all to himself.

Once Betty and I went to a specialty shop and bought Carol's two girls, Morgan and Timmy Lynn, and Faye's daughter, Lilly, the cutest little dresses. Ruffles all the way down. The girls were so happy to get them. All three wore them for us, so proud of them, but they looked awful. They had to be three sizes too big. We took these little dresses to Utah anyway, because the girls were pleased with them, but Betty and I felt so disappointed.

Managing a Crisis. When Faye had been in Utah for a while and her kids were getting bigger, I began to get anxious to see the family. I went to the phone thinking she would be pleased for me to come see her. I was giving her plenty of notice; my projected date, May 16, was still six weeks away. Her answer was, "I have something to tell you, and you might not want to come see me after you hear." I thought, what could be so terrible that I would not want to come see her. "What is happening," I asked. She said, "I am expecting a baby girl that day." What to say!!! I surely did not want to hurt her feelings. I loved all my grandchildren. I stammered, I stuttered, "Well, that's great." Then almost immediately I said, "I have to get off the phone, I have a headache."

Mama had had 13, but Faye did not have the health that some women do. I felt for her more then she could possibly know. She had a thyroid that barely worked, even though she had been on medicine for a long time. She had lots of health problems.

I was aware of my tendency to overreact, and I did. My first thought: I will just jump off a cliff. Next thought: No, I can't do that, she may need me. I have to do something. I cannot just sit here. I know, I will shave my head; my hair was bothering me anyway. I went to the bathroom, grabbed a pair of scissors and started in on my hair. When I finished, my hair was about an inch long. When I went to the playroom where Betty and Kay were, Kay exclaimed, "Aunt Catherine, what have you done to your hair?" I informed them that I had reacted a little impulsively; then I broke the news.

Kay had a suggestion to improve my state of mind. The next time I went to town, I was to buy a little something pink for the new baby; that would get me started planning and thinking positive thoughts about the baby, and I would not worry as much. That is what I did. Every time I went to town, I bought something pink. Pink blanket. Pink dresses. Pink everything. I acquired a complete pink wardrobe for the new little girl.

I joined Faye on her due date, but the baby was not on time. Her doctor had to be out of town and had arranged for a substitute doctor. When she went into labor at home, she was not acting her normal self. She knew something was wrong; she had had babies before, after all. She was having unproductive labor. I was ready for an emergency, but Larry, being calmer, suggested he give her a blessing. Which he did. Then her labor became fast and hard. I knew that if her water broke, that baby would be born in the car. Larry got in the back seat with her as a precaution; I drove and – I promise you – it did not take us 30 minutes to go that 30 miles to the hospital in Delta. We barely got to the delivery room – I was just outside the door, and almost immediately heard the announcement, "You have a big baby boy." All I could think was: Pink? PINK!! Thus poor Will had to wear pink home from the hospital.

Day Care

Betty, who had kept kids before, had encouraged me to go into day care. I told her I was too far out in the country – outside of West Plains – to be successful. She suggested that I run an ad and see what would happen. Just to pacify her, I did. The very day the ad came out, a grandmother stopped at my house to inquire. She enrolled her four-year-old grandson, who lived two miles from me. Quickly, I began to fill up with kids. After a while, I separated my living quarters from the day care and became licensed. Betty moved nearby and added a day care of her own fairly close to mine. We quickly developed a reputation for being very good with the kids, and soon we were both full up. Our whole life was tied up with day care, but what little spare time we had, Betty and I spent together.

I hired a very good helper who was super-special with kids. The parent of my very first enrolled child, Shane Eades, added another child, Cody, who was seven weeks old. In time, she added another child, Shad, at four weeks old. As they grew, I had them after school and in the summer as well. I felt like I practically raised the Eades boys.

Special Memories. One day I was in day care doing my thing, and I saw a truck drive up. This tall handsome boy got out with two younger boys. He walked in and looked at me with a big smile on his face. I just looked at him. Then he said, "You don't know me, do you? I am Shane Eades." Wow. I jumped up and gave him a big hug. My very first child that I had enrolled in day care! With him were his brothers, Shad and Cody. They told me they had been over in town and had started talking about me, and wanted to come see me. They stayed for the next hour and we reminisced. I knew that I had created special memories for these boys, and it left me with a very good feeling.

The Hot Dog Rule. Children love hot dogs usually, which we served often. I had a rule that hot dogs had to be cut up. I had a great-nephew who had choked to death on a hot dog, which made me very cautious about them. One day, Shane's mother told me she had served hot dogs the day before. Her son had informed her she did not do it right; she had to cut them up first. She thought this was humorous but she did cut them up before she served them. We were careful about every child's health, so I was pleased to see my rule practiced.

Sarah

One day I came in after doing some shopping and Tom told me he had some good news and some bad news. I immediately asked about the good news. He said Matt had got his call to go on his mission and that he was going to Canada. I was super happy. After a while I asked about the bad news. He said he thought Faye was pregnant again. Now I have to explain – again – that we loved all of our grandchildren very much, but were terribly afraid for Faye. Her health since a little girl had been bad. We had almost lost her with her first baby, so this news had us on edge. I asked him how he knew and he said Matt told him. Matt had not been able to get his driver's license because his mother was too nervous to teach him to drive. She was nervous because she was pregnant. He was glad, though, that he would get to be there when the baby was born.

This was all news to me. I felt she was too old to have a baby. Apparently, being 45 did not stop her. I knew of course why Faye did not tell me she was pregnant. I was such a worrier and probably made her feel bad about it, but I only wanted the best for everyone. Sarah was the only child whose birth I could not attend. She was born before Matt went on his mission. I really do not want to send any grandchildren back, and I am sure glad Mama had me – even though I was number 12.

Day Care Plus

I could not help it. After Sarah, I felt left out and hurt and anxious. You name it, I felt it. Tom was taking so much out of me at the time. I was keeping up with day care, including taking college classes required for day care. Even though he was not well, Tom was attending college classes with me. Whereas he had always been the A student, now he needed *my* help. My plate was full.

I began to believe that I needed a computer. With help from more knowledgeable people, I found a place that built my computer for me. I am so thankful for that, because my grandkids and many others learned to use the computer in my house. Back then, even most libraries did not use a computer. In our community, we were some of the first to learn.

The computer was especially helpful in my genealogy work. I had always been involved in tracing my family history and wishing I had more time for it. It was truly a passion and was always at the back of my mind. Sometimes, I felt like a driven woman. I had sent away for many birth and death certificates and done as much as I could. Then along came Judy.

Judy

Virginia's daughter Judy did wonderful things in genealogy. I felt so thankful for her. She made friends with another person who was working on the same line. Together they made a trip to Salt Lake Family History Library and made amazing connections within the Mooney line. I shall always be grateful for all our ancestors that she gathered up. She traced people many generations back and into other countries. She loved the work so much, she volunteered at the local LDS genealogy center during the week, even though she was not a church member.

Blessings

I started getting involved in church again and had church members over regularly. One weekend, Faye and Larry were visiting and they attended our ward. I was working in primary and three of her boys were there. In the opening exercise we sang songs. One of the songs was "Give, Said the Little Stream." After we sang it, Matthieu held his hand up and asked the instructor, "Do you sing it in French?" Her answer was "No, do you?" Matt said, "My brothers and I do," so she asked them to sing it in French. Those three little boys got up in front of everyone and sang: "Give, Said the Little Stream" in French. If I had been wearing a shirt with buttons, I would have burst them all. I was so proud. They sang another song in French, but it was not as impressive. Their dad, who had served his mission in France, had taught his kids well.

Tom was beginning to get involved also. He had visitors from church call on him and he attended some meetings. He still was having a coffee and cigarette problem, but he was trying to do the right things. By then, he was diabetic and had a very bad heart. To our dismay, his doctor informed him if he tried to quit smoking, he might have a heart attack – not what we wanted to hear.

After a visit we had with the bishop and the president over the priesthood, as they walked out the door, they took me aside and told me Tom had asked for a special blessing to be able to quit smoking. Shock to me. He always kept things to himself. Well, guess what? Tom ended up in the hospital with heart failure the following Saturday. He was given a blessing and told that he had been given a second chance to get his house in order. He came home from the hospital with no desire for a cigarette.

I can easily say that the best years of our marriage were the last three. Tom was not always well enough to attend church, but most times he was there. Until then, he had not received the Aaronic or Melchizedek priesthoods. He gained both and we started attending a seminar to get us ready for the temple. By this time, you could go without your spouse, but I never did; so it was my first temple recommend also.

The Temple

Salt Lake City. Even though I was fully active in church, I never thought to tell my bishop that we were almost ready for the temple. I guess we thought we had to do it all ourselves. We finished our class and got our temple recommend. Tom said he had always liked the Salt Lake Temple, so we made plans to go. We called the temple and arranged to be sealed for time and all eternity. We also took our parents' information with us.

Our kids met us at the temple, along with Betty's daughter Carol, who lived close by. Even as I write, it brings tears to my eyes, the greatness of it all. I had waited so long for Tom to get ready. Larry was there for Tom. Faye was there for me. Betty's daughters Kay and Carol were with us too. We got a suite at the Marriott Hotel and both my girls were there. We had contacted the missionary couple who had taught Tom, and they were there also. They lived in Utah nearby. Elder Ken Olkerson was the one who had baptized Tom in 1981. He had worked in the Salt Lake Temple, so Tom requested his friend to be our sealer. We really had so much work done. We were sealed for time and all eternity June 3, 1993. We were sealed to each other and to our parents. Our parents were sealed to one another and to any children that had passed on. It was so very emotional that even the sealer had tears in his eyes. We spent three days having all our work done. Our kids went back to their homes. We turned our car in and found our way back to the airport to return home.

Jill, the girl that took over for me, had brought her family to stay in our house so we could go. I do love Jill Shaw, who did so much to help us in every way. I shall be thankful for her all of my days.

We went back to church and everyone seemed so surprised that we had been to temple. I suppose we should have discussed it with more people. Having day care, though, I did not have much visiting time, and Tom took a big part of my time as well.

Dallas. Tom had to have regular monthly treatments for his heart and was in the hospital for a few days each time. He was in the hospital for one of his treatments when I got a call from the Dallas temple. The clerk told me that the temple president wanted to talk to us; when could we come down? I told him Tom was in the hospital and I would have to check with him. He said he would call me back Saturday. We calculated when we thought Tom would feel the best after his treatment and set a date.

It had hardly been a month since we had been to the Salt Lake Temple. I guess my head was not on very straight, because I really did not understand the purpose of this visit. I knew that we did a lot of genealogy, so I thought his request had something to do with genealogy. I must have dismissed any other possibility from my mind.

Our bishop was at our house soon afterward, and I mentioned our call from the Dallas temple. I told him they wanted us to go to Dallas. His eyes lit up and he said, "I would listen if I were you. They have a direct line."

After the clerk made an appointment for us, we started preparing for the trip. We flew there and rented a car. Tom was on oxygen by then, so everything we did was difficult. I thought I was going to lose him once when we had to walk so far out into the rental car lot. They were so busy there, they could not help us properly. Dallas is a big city, and we had gotten used to the country by then, so we bought a map to help us find our way to the temple. When we went inside, Tom did not take his oxygen, but should have.

It was all unreal to us. We were uncertain about where to go and what to do. The person at the front desk called someone, who took us immediately to the temple president's office. I will never forget L. Lynol Kendricks. He sat us down and told us we had been called to be temple workers. Tom put his fist on the desk and said to President Kendricks, "It's like this, I have never really done anything in the church." The reply, "Brother Henson, it is not how you come into the world, it is how you go out." Tom said, "Well, I am going out right." And he did exactly that. The temple president said to his assistant, "We have a sick man here that we need to put to work. Heavenly Father has sent him here; it is up to us to make a place for him." We had been set apart for temple work and we began to make our plans.

We knew that our day care would not allow us to work full time, so a plan was made for us to work one week out of every month. Jill and her family moved into our house each time we worked at the temple. The ten-hour drive was not easy, but it was a joy. We had Monday to prepare and get there. I had cassette tapes of the Old Testament, and we listened to them while I drove. We also had the Book of Mormon in story form, called *The Hallowed Journey*. Those tapes helped us on each trip.

The joy that we experienced from temple work was incredible. My husband, who had always been a little on the gruff side, turned into an almost angelic human being. I really felt like it was his calling more then mine. He developed such a love for the temple and all it represented. We were not the same people any more. Tom, who was not a smiley person, seemed to always wear a little smile on his face.

We worked almost a year until Tom's health began to get worse. I was told by the doctors that he had only so much time. I had to call the temple and say we could not come back. Tom got so upset with me. He was not ready to give up the temple. Larry and Faye moved back to Missouri to be with us, which was a very good thing. Tom had said, "I know all my grandchildren but Sarah, and I need to know her, and she needs to know me." She was ten months old when they returned. Sarah really took to her granddad. Every time we moved him, she would ride in the wheelchair with him and squeal with delight.

A Visit From Vida

One day a few months earlier, I had fixed Betty's hair and she was under the hair dryer in my bedroom. When she was dry, she came into the living room and sat down on the couch with a troubled look on her face – kind of staring into the distance. Finally, she said to me, "Vida just visited me." It's important to note here that Vida had passed away over 20 years ago, a few months before Mama.

Betty said they carried on a conversation, but she could remember only parts of it. She said Vida was sitting in a chair across from her....*where there was no chair*. When Vida got up to leave, Betty said to her, "Don't go." Vida told her she had to go, but she would be back. Betty was getting the impression that she would be coming back to escort someone to the other side. In that moment, Betty thought she herself might be going to die, but she was wrong. Vida said again, "I will be back soon."

Tom's Death

Even though Tom was so sick, he was easy to be around. He was a good patient. On one of his stays in the hospital, Faye wanted me to see the house they had bought. Knowing the nurses would look out for him, we drove to her house, which was about an hour away. We were on our way home when Tom called, wanting to know where we were. All the way home he kept calling. I hurried as fast as I could to get there. I was grateful that I had a car phone by then, because there were no cell phones available yet. When we rushed into the hospital, the nurse called me aside. The doctor had said I should stay, that there was danger of Tom's passing away that night. The nurse made me a bed to sleep in, and I spent the night in his room. Tom was resilient, though. He made it through the night and went home again.

I knew that I was going to lose Tom and it really worked on my nerves. It is very hard waiting for your spouse to die. Sometimes you just want to say...*When*?!!!!!!!!!! Along about that time, Tom was given another blessing. He was told that he had completed his mission. Heavenly Father was pleased with him, and he was ready to go.

I still had day care, but could not spend much time there. Fortunately, I had plenty of help. Faye was filling in for me. She was a real comfort. She had a deep understanding for me and her dad. I really do not know how I would have held up, had it not been for her and our grandchildren.

Every time Dan or Nick went through the room, they went over and gave their granddad a big hug. He never went to bed during the day. He always sat at the dining table. Matthieu was away on his mission, and Josh could not be there either. Every morning, Tom would ask, "Where are my boys?" It meant so much to him to have his grandchildren around.

The hospice nurses had taught me how to give him his meds as well as his shots. He had a portacath that I administered meds into each day. Hospice was calling on him every day and Tom knew he was not going to make it. He wondered about the Mormon funeral rites, since he had never been to one. He told me when Howard W. Hunter (our LDS President) died, to record his funeral. I did record it, although he never watched it. I still have it.

Ann had made a couple of trips home for her dad when he had not been expected to make it, but he got better each time. For some reason, it was not his time yet. His trips to the hospital had stopped since hospice was calling on him. We were all feeling very stressed with the waiting.

One morning, a new hospice nurse appeared at my door just as I had fixed Tom's breakfast. He was sitting at his favorite place at the dining table, ready to eat. She examined him, picked up his foot and said to me, as if he wasn't there, "He has started the dying process; see, his foot has started muddling." Tom pushed his breakfast back and just sat there. I wanted to throw her out the door – she could have talked to me in private. I still feel she was a little off-base.

Later, I picked up his foot to see what she was talking about, and he yanked it out of my hand. He still sat at the dining table. After a while, we got him to his recliner. In a few more hours, he was leaning sideways in the chair. Faye and I talked him into the hospital bed. It had been in our living room for a couple of months, but he had never gotten into that bed. The kids and I had taken a nap or two in it, but never Tom.

Faye urged me to go take a nap because it might be a long night. I had barely begun to doze when Faye called me. When I got back in the room, Tom was speaking kind of blurred-like. He was talking to his uncle Harley. And he also was calling Vida's name. Several times, he repeated her name. He had been close to Vida and had been to her rescue a number of times. I truly felt like she had come for him. Tom died November 21, 1995, the day before Thanksgiving.

We were waiting for the coroner to come. It had been a hard thing for us all, but we were accepting it. I noticed Lilly was in the kitchen washing dishes, and she never quit working. I guess that was her way of coping. Dan went to the shop and started making a plaque honoring his granddad – using his granddad's welder. As for myself, I knew that I needed day care and to be around those little children, so 11 days later we were back in business. We all held it together in our own ways.

After the funeral, the sweetest spirit stayed in my house for a few days. When one of the kids would argue, it would leave, but it came back. That was a comfort to me. That peaceful spirit was what got me through. The only place I could not stay in was the dining room where he always sat; I was too emotional at first. When I went into the dining room, to me he was still there. The chair he sat in at the table was still his. When we had dinner, nobody took granddad's chair. Finally, after several months, one of the kids said, "Well, I will just sit here." We all laughed because we had been thinking the same thing.

Matthieu came home from his mission still upset because he had missed his granddad's funeral. I understood how deeply his death had affected his grandchildren.

While some people might have trouble sleeping in the bed they had shared with their newly-departed spouse, that was not at all my problem. I had always been in the bed long before Tom. In the last few months, he wouldn't go to bed at all. If I were going to be disturbed by sensing his presence anywhere, it would not have been the bed. I felt his presence most at the dining room table, where he sat most of the time before he died; and that came to be a source of great comfort to me. Even though the love of my life was gone, he was certainly not forgotten. He was still with us all.

Swimming Pool

I had always wanted a swimming pool, so about ten months after Tom's death, I had a pool put in. It was 18 x 40 feet. A very nice pool. My grandkids loved it so much, as we all did. It provided us lots of healing family time.

Sarah took to the pool like she was a duck. First thing we did was train her to wear floaters. We were a big family again. I believe the pool was the best thing to bring us all back to life. We swam at night, day, any time we chose. It really gave us so much pleasure. Not just for my grandkids, but for my day care kids too. I had to have a licensed lifeguard in order to take the day care kids in. So Jill went to school to become a lifeguard, and it worked out well. There was really no danger anyway, because we would not let the little ones around the pool without lifejackets on.

Some days when the kids got grumpy and nothing made them happy, I would say, "Time for swimming!" It was amazing how their attitudes changed from grumpy to happy. So many little kids learned to swim that would not have otherwise. We did more crafts and teaching in the winter when it was too cold for the pool. We really did have happy kids.

Faye had moved farther away, but she was still at my house a lot. We always kept the pool gate locked when day care was in progress, which was Monday through Friday. One weekend when Faye was there, we had all been swimming that morning, but we were sure we had locked the gates afterward. When Faye and I were fixing lunch, we looked out the kitchen window, and there was Sarah in the pool all alone. She might have been three years, or almost. We both panicked and headed for the pool. Fortunately, Sarah knew the routine. She had gone out, put on her floaters and got in – the only thing that saved her. Right then and there we told her, you have to learn to swim. Her brothers took her out and swam beside her until she would get tired and say, "hand me a stick." We kept sticks in the water; they worked as life preservers. By the end of the summer, she knew how to swim.

If I had it to do all over again, I would have put that pool in when we moved there. It was late in life for me – I was 72 – but it did the trick for me. I had overcome my lonesomeness and started having fun again.

Life After Tom

After my husband had been dead about a year, I had a friend who wanted to introduce me to her father-in-law. I met him and we attended a few seniors dances. As a result, I got interested in making myself attractive again. We dated for a little while, but after the new wore off, I enjoyed talking to him over the phone more than dating him. I was losing interest. However, my grandsons did not know that I was losing interest, so one day they ganged up on me to tell me what they thought. Each one told me what he would do if I married Roy. I cannot remember all they said. Matthieu, who was still mourning his granddad's death, said, "Grandma, If you marry Roy, I won't come see you anymore." I knew they all loved me. All I could do was laugh; I could not believe those boys.

There was also an ex-postal employee who became interested in me. His name was Norman. He wanted to come out and visit me one day. It was during work hours, so I had my employees take over in day care. I told him I would be out by the pool. After he arrived, we were just relaxing and visiting in lounging chairs by the pool. It was a very pleasant setting. Then the patio door opened and there was Nick, and into the pool he jumped. The patio door opened again, and out came Dan and he jumped into the pool. I looked at Norman, he looked at me, and we both just laughed. Neither of us needed a chaperone. We never went out, except to dinner once.

Next I was introduced to a gentleman who had just moved into our ward. His name was Herman. He was more interesting to me than the others, and we talked of getting married, much to the distress of my grandsons. We went to a few dances at the seniors club. He would pick me up and we would attend church together. Then he would bring me home, I would cook lunch, and by late afternoon he would be gone. I had that same relaxed feeling with him that I had with Tom, and I liked him, but I was having doubts.

Ann had asked me not to get married before she took her vacation in the summer. She always slept with me in my king-size bed during her vacations. As she requested, I did not consider any wedding dates before her time to come home. She said it would be her last time to get to sleep with me in the big bed.

Herman began to talk of moving away to another town after we married. Now I already knew that I would not do that. As it turned out, that was an issue that we didn't need to resolve. Our next date was to be at the senior center on Tuesday evening, but he dropped dead from a heart attack the night before. Right there and then I said: No more. I am not going through that again. That was the end of my interest in getting remarried.

Now my four grandsons that were so concerned about me getting married should have worried about themselves. All but one is still single. They should have been more like me – I had at least considered getting married.

An interesting thing happened when Ann came home for her vacation. That first night home, she went to another bedroom and started getting ready for bed. I was shocked, considering the big plea she had made earlier. I asked, "Are you sleeping in that room?" Her answer was, "Yes, I can use the fan in here." It wasn't that I cared where she slept, but I went to bed knowing that she didn't even remember what she had asked.

I spent the next five years in day care, but I was getting older, and day care was becoming less interesting. Faye had moved away, Dan was on his mission in Japan, and I was spending most of my weekends going to see Betty in Conway. So when someone made me a good offer on my house and day care business, I took it and moved out, all within a three-week period. I had to give up my nice house and pool, which bothered all my grandkids, but they were not around to keep me company when I was lonely. I bought a lesser house in Conway close to Betty and one street over from her daughter Carol. I actually bought it more because of its location near the family than its condition. It kept me busy trying to fix it up nice, but even so, I had time to visit with people again.

I went to Oregon to see Ann. While I was there, her lady boss, Sherri, asked me if I would stay and take care of her mother, who had moved into an elegant retirement home. I would have my own bedroom and was needed only for companionship. That sounded good, so I accepted and stayed there a year. After a while, when I began to need my own home again, I left and moved back to Arkansas.

It is not my nature to be inactive; soon after I came home, I began to look at different things I could do. I saw an ad in the paper for caregivers for seniors. I answered that ad and was hired immediately. It was a new business and I was the fifth person hired. I knew I did not look my age, which was important to getting the job. So when I filled out my application for employment, I kind of carelessly messed up the age part. I surely was not about to tell him I was 80. After being hired and ready to go, the boss asked for my driver's license to make a copy. I saw him do a double-take. His head sort of jerked back, like a surprised jerk, but he didn't comment.

I ended up being one of his treasured employees. I did 24-hour senior care. I received several awards and was nominated for Caregiver for the Nation award. I did not get that, but I was first in our area, and I had several write-ups in the newspaper.

About my service as a caregiver, there is a saying that as you get older, you get more child-like. Having been in day care so long helped me in senior care. It became natural with me. It is just as easy to love a senior as it is to love a child.

I stayed at the last assignment for a long time. Due to my age, the company might not have sent me out anymore, so I knew it could be my last job. The only reason I was there so long was because my patient had Alzheimer's and his two daughters wanted me to stay on with him. When I had started, he was always hunting for his wife. Soon afterwards, he became comfortable with me and stopped hunting for her. Maybe my age helped, as I was a year older than he. He was a real gentleman. He had a degree in forestry that hung on his wall. We went out to lunch every day, as he had when his wife was alive. I tried to make him comfortable in every way. I was there five years. The last year, he was sicker and could not get out of bed. I only worked three 24-hour days at the last. Hospice was calling on him by then. I had reached my 88th birthday that November. By that time, I had needed to go on oxygen. My client, James Donald Mabry, died November 23, 2012.

I had become a friend to his daughters, Laura and Lisa Williams, especially Lisa. Lisa helped me as well, and I was grateful. Soon after Mr. Mabry died, the daughters had a Christmas party for his two caregivers and presented each of us with a $1,000 bonus check. I deeply appreciated this expression of their love and caring. I did not expect that.

Even though I am 91 now, I still keep my own house and do my own driving. My girls are in other states, but I have one grandson who lives with me. I do think you should not wait until you are 91 to start a book, but I did. I hope this book will interest my family and will provide knowledge they wouldn't otherwise have.

APPENDIX A

Franklin M. Mooney Family History

1 Franklin M. MOONEY[1]

Birth: 29 Nov 1840, TN[2]
Death: 1863[3]
Father: Boaz "Bose" MOONEY (1813-1865)
Mother: Elizabeth (1817-1888)

Spouse: Elizabeth A. WIDENER
Birth: 1839, GA
Death: 1874[4]
Father: Moses Perry WIDENER (1817- >1900)
Mother: Martha C. DYER (1819->1870)

Children: James Franklin Marion Jackson (1863-1940)

1.1a James Franklin Marion Jackson MOONEY*

Birth: 5 May 1863, KY[3,5,6]
Death: 21 Feb 1940, Dell, AR[7]
Burial: Blytheville, AR (Elmwood Cem)

Spouse: Sarah Jane PETERSON
Birth: ca 1856, AR[8]
Death: aft 1896, AR
Father: Jno PETERSON (1831-)
Mother: Mary Jane ROSS (1821-)
Marr: 19 Nov 1882, Miss Co, AR[9]

Children: Mary Elizabeth (1883-1923)

1.1a.1 Mary Elizabeth MOONEY

Birth: 27 Sep 1883, AR[10]
Death: 2 Feb 1923[10]
Burial: Mound Cemetery, Dell, AR

Spouse: John August KOEHLER
Birth: 9 Feb 1865[10]
Death: 13 Nov 1926[10]

Father:	H KOEHLER (1826-)
Mother:	Annie
Marr:	30 Jul 1899, Luxora, AR[11]

Children:	Susie (1899-1900)
	Baby Herman (1901-1902)
	Otto (1903-~1997)
	J. Merron (1906-)
	Rachel (1907-)
	August (1908-1909)
	Mildred (1912-)
	Raymond (1913-)
	J. Herman (1915-)
	Baby Lily (1917-1917)
	Thelma Louise (1918-)

1.1b James Franklin Marion Jackson MOONEY* (See above)

Spouse:	Laura GARDNER
Birth:	Mar 1867, TN
Marr:	13 Jul 1889, Mississippi Co, AR[12]

1.1c James Franklin Marion Jackson MOONEY* (See above)

Spouse:	Josephine RAY
Birth:	23 Jan 1887, Dell, Ark[13]
Death:	20 Feb 1973, Dell, Ark[13]
Father:	Anderson "Bud" RAY (ca1854-<1900)
Mother:	Anna Jane EDDINGS (1865-1935)
Marr:	20 Jul 1904, Dell, AR[14]

Children:	Stella (1905-1993)
	Willie (1907-1932)
	Franklin (1909-1915)
	Magaline Miranda "Johnnie" (1910-1994)
	Lloyd James (1912-1939)
	Anna Cassie (1914-2004)
	Floyd Jackson "Bud" (1916-2006)
	Wilma Pauline (1918-)
	Velma Virginia (1920-1996)
	Vida Ray (1921-1972)
	Mary Lee (1923-2008)

Catherine
Betty Jo

1.1c.1 Stella MOONEY

Birth:	3 Oct 1905, Dell, AR[15]
Death:	19 Jan 1993, Florala, AL[15]
Burial:	Blytheville, AR

Spouse:	Kirby John COOK
Birth:	1902, TN[15]
Marr:	29 Aug 1921, Dell, Mississippi, AR

Children: Kirby James "K.J."
Josey
Syble
LaVern
Clydell
Grace
Billy Jack
Patricia
Jean
Jerry
Tom
Carolyn
Janet

1.1c.2 Willie MOONEY

Birth:	2 Jul 1907, Dell, AR[15]
Death:	2 Dec 1932, Albuquerque, NM[15]
Burial:	Albuquerque, NM

Spouse:	Doc Hull WELLS
Birth:	30 May 1901[15]
Death:	21 Feb 1978[15]
Marr:	15 Jul 1925[15]

Children: Maryan Ruth
Melroy
Thomas Mooney
Billy Delbert
Malcolm Keith

1.1c.3 Franklin MOONEY

Birth: 10 Jan 1909, Ravenden Springs, Randolph, AR[15]
Death: 3 Aug 1915, Ravenden Springs, Randolph, AR[15]

1.1c.4a Magaline Miranda "Johnnie" MOONEY*

Birth: 22 Oct 1910, Ravenden Springs, Randolph Co, AR[16]
Death: 2 Aug 1994, Blytheville, AR[16]
Burial: Blytheville, AR

Spouse: Louis Bryan TURNER
Birth: 1 Aug 1896, Ridgely, Lake, TN[16]
Death: 13 Feb 1965, Chicago, Cook, IL[16]
Father: Alonzo L. TURNER
Mother: Pearl BRYAN
Marr: 15 Jul 1926, Randolph Co, AR[16]

Children: Mary Elizabeth
                    Louise Woodard
                    Barnard
                    Vicki Dale

1.1c.4b Magaline Miranda "Johnnie" MOONEY* (See above)

Spouse: Shelby BYRD
Death: 4 Apr 1977, Memphis TN[16]
Marr: 1 Jun 1952, Greene Co AR[16]

1.1c.5 Lloyd James MOONEY

Birth: 12 Feb 1912, Ravenden Springs, AR
Death: 5 Jun 1939, Dell, Miss Co, AR[6]
Burial: Elmwood Cemetery, Blytheville, AR

Spouse: Lola HUDSON

Children: Jimmy A

1.1c.6 Anna Cassie MOONEY

Birth:	23 Apr 1914, Ravenden Springs, AR[17]
Death:	30 Dec 2004, Smithville, Craighead Co, AR[17]

Spouse:	Clarence GRICE
Birth:	23 Mar 1911, IL[17]
Death:	13 Dec 1972, Batesville AR[17]
Father:	Wiley GRICE
Mother:	Bertha RAY
Marr:	13 Sep 1931, Miss Co. AR

Children:	Peggy
	Barbara

1.1c.7a Floyd Jackson "Bud" MOONEY*

Birth:	5 Dec 1916, Ravenden Springs, Randolph, AR[15]
Death:	7 Dec 2006, Carthage, TX[15]
Burial:	10 Dec 2006, Oddfellows Cemetery

Spouse:	Pansy EVANS

Children:	Gene
	Jimmy

1.1c.7b Floyd Jackson "Bud" MOONEY* (See above)

Spouse:	Mildred EADES

Children:	Rebecca Ann
	Jackson

1.1c.7c Floyd Jackson "Bud" MOONEY* (See above)

Spouse:	Annie Marie MINYARD
Death:	1 Nov 2004, Carthage, TX[15]
Marr:	6 Aug 1977[15]

Children:	Janet

1.1c.8 Wilma Pauline MOONEY

Birth:	8 Aug 1918, Dell, AR[15]
Spouse:	John Robert HENDERSON
Birth:	7 May 1914, Dell, AR[15]
Death:	9 Oct 1988, Torrance, CA[15]
Father:	James Vance HENDERSON (1887-)
Mother:	Maggie MORGAN (1892-)
Marr:	27 Dec 1941, Dell, AR[15]
Children:	John Robert
	James Franklin

1.1c.9 Velma Virginia MOONEY

Birth:	12 Mar 1920, Ravenden Springs, AR[18]
Death:	15 Sep 1996, Blytheville, AR[19]
Burial:	18 Sep 1996, Elmwood Cemetery
Spouse:	Carl MARTIN
Birth:	6 May 1914, Sunflower, MS[20]
Death:	20 Nov 1985, Memphis, TN[21]
Father:	William Walter "Doc" MARTIN (1877-1941)
Mother:	Tabor Louise LITTLE (1878-1954)
Marr:	2 Sep 1942, Kennett, MO[22]
Children:	Judy Virginia

1.1c.10 Vida Ray MOONEY

Birth:	11 Nov 1921, Ravenden Springs, Randolph Co, AR[15]
Death:	21 Jun 1972, Forrest City, AR[15]
Spouse:	Haywood HOLSCLAW
Children:	Donna Ray
	Jimmy

1.1c.11 Mary Lee MOONEY

Birth: 2 May 1923, Ravenden Springs, AR[23]
Death: 3 Jun 2008, Keiser, Miss.Co, AR[15]

Spouse: Calvin Buford JARRETT
Birth: 11 Sep 1913[23]
Death: 9 Aug 1989, Keiser, AR[23]
Father: Curn Levan JARRETT
Mother: Florence
Marr: 16 Jun 1941, Blytheville, Mississippi, AR

Children: Melody
                      Sandra
                      Calvin Buford "Jerry"

1.1c.12 Catherine MOONEY

Birth: 28 Nov 1924, Ravenden Springs , AR[15]

Spouse: Thomas Eugene "Red" HENSON
Birth: 20 Mar 1924, Clear Lake AR[24]
Death: 21 Nov 1995, West Plains, MO[24]
Father: Louis Oliver HENSON
Mother: Lilly Agathabelle LOVELADY
Marr: 20 Apr 1947, Blytheville, Mississippi, AR[24]

Children: Kathryn Ann
                      Carolyn Faye

1.1c.13 Betty Jo MOONEY

Birth: 18 May 1927, Ravenden Springs, AR[15]

Spouse: Alvin Gaston TAYLOR
Marr: Mar 1951, Mississippi Co, AR

Children: Fred
                      Phina Kay
                      Suzanne
                      Carol Lee
                      Timothy R.

END NOTES

1. Muster roll, 4th Confederate Regiment Alabama Cavalry, 22 September 1862, copy of original in National Archives. Has Franklin's middle initial 'M'.

2. Family Bible of Martha Breshears Beatty, Bert Beatty, Muskogee,Oklahoma. Martha was the daughter of Pierce Mooney, the youngest son of Boaz Mooney. The information is from a copy of the Bible ma32de by Norene Dearmore, also a descendant of Pierce Mooney.

3. Death of Franklin Mooney and birth of James F Mooney: The 1863 death date is supported by the following: Franklin's only child, James Franklin, was born May 5, 1863, although some documents say 1862. Franklin enlisted 6 Sep 1862. According to family tradition, he deserted and was present at his son's birth but died not long after. A muster roll (4th Confederate Regiment Alabama Cavalry, 22 Sep 1862, copy of original in National Archives), shows that Franklin was still alive 22 Sep 1862. If James F. were born May 1862, his father would not yet be a soldier; therefore the most likely birthdate is May 1863. By the same reasoning, Franklin's death was most likely in 1863.

4. Death of Elizabeth Widener Mooney: Exact date and place of Elizabeth's death are not known. James F. told his children he was 12 when she died. The year of her death is based on that assertion.

5. Birthplace of James F Mooney: Although census records say James F. was born in Alabama, his daughter Catherine Henson says that he told her he was born in Kentucky and, as informant on Lloyd's death certificate, he said Kentucky.

6. Lloyd J. Mooney Death Certificate No. 685, photocopy of original, Dell, Mississippi County, Arkansas; Bureau of Vital Statistics, Arkansas Board of Health. Informant: J.F. Mooney.

7. James F. Mooney Death Certificate No. 969, certified copy, Dell, Hector County, Arkansas; Bureau of Vital Statistics, Arkansas State Board of Health. Informant: Mrs. Josephine Mooney.

8. Jno Peterson household, Sarah Jane Peterson, p. 27, dwelling 110, family 108, 1880 federal census, Mississippi County, Arkansas (filmed). National Archives T9-51. Family History Library, Salt Lake City, Utah.

9. J.F. Mooney-Jennie Peterson marriage record, 19 November 1882, Mississippi County courthouse, Osceola, Arkansas. Marriage Volume 4, 454.

10. Information from Thelma Louise Crawford, daughter of August Koehler and Elizabeth Mooney.

11. Augustus Koehler-Elizabeth Mooney marriage. Photocopy of original at Mississippi County courthouse, Osceola, Arkansas. Book 10, no page number.

License 28 July 1899, married 30 July 1899, recorded 13 September 1899. Both parties resided in Luxora, Mississippi County, Arkansas.

12. Marriage of J.F. Mooney-Laura Gardner, 13 July 1889, Mississippi Co, Arkansas, Book 5, p. 425, Photocopy, Mississippi Co, Arkansas County Courthouse. Both resided in Big Lake, Mississippi Co.

13. Josephine Mooney Minyard Cemetery Inscription. January 23, 1887 to February 20, 1973, Elmwood Cemetery, Blytheville, Arkansas.

14. Marriage of J.F. Mooney-Josephine Ray, 17 Jul 1904, Mississippi Co, Arkansas, Vol A, p. 441, Mississippi County and Probate Court. License 16 July 1904; married 17 July 1904; recorded 20 Jul 1904.

15. Catherine Henson, "James Franklin Mooney-Josephine Ray family group sheet," supplied in 1997.

16. Louise Turner Boyle, "Johnnie Mooney-Bryan Turner family group sheet," supplied 26 June 1998.

17. Peggy Stephens, "Clarence Grice-Anna Cassie Mooney family group sheet," supplied 28 June 1998.

18. Velma Virginia Mooney Delayed Birth Certificate No. 3658, signed by Josephine Mooney 23 February 1954; Arkansas State Board of Health, issued 25 February 1954.

19. Velma Virginia Martin Death Certificate, 237734, 96.018915, Arkansas Department of Health, filed 2 October 1996.

20. Personal knowledge of daughter.

21. Carl S. Martin Death Certificate No. 85-045632, Office of Vital Records, Tennessee. Informant: Wife Virginia Martin.

22. Carl Martin-Virginia Mooney Marriage Certificate; signed by Justice of the Peace, J. A. Lane; issued 2 September 1842 by Dunklin County, Missouri Recorder of Deeds.

23. Mary Lee Jarrett, "Calvin Buford Jarrett-Mary Lee Mooney family group sheet," supplied 28 June 1998.

24. Catherine Henson, "Thomas Henson-Catherine Mooney family group sheet," supplied in 1997.

Prepared by Judy Underwood

APPENDIX B

The Early Mooneys

Sampson Mooney is our oldest verifiable Mooney ancestor. He was born in Virginia in 1793 and appears on the tax list for Grayson County, VA in 1810. He and his older brothers Charles and William migrated to White County, TN well before 1820. Charles and William married sisters, Francis and Lucinda Hayse/Hayes in Grainger County, TN in 1807 and 1804 respectively. There was also a John Mooney who stayed in Grayson County who was most likely another brother. Sampson and his probable brothers and their wives are shown below:

Unknown MOONEY
| **John MOONEY**
       bd. abt 1775, VA
| & Sarah STONEMAN
       bd. 1786, NC
| **Charles MOONEY**
       bd. abt 1780, VA
       dd. after 1850, Morgan Co, AL
| & Francis (HAYSE?)
       bd. abt 1780, VA?
| **William MOONEY**
       bd. Abt 1785, VA
       dd. aft 1860, Yalobusha Co, MS
| & Lucinda HAYSE
       & Catherine Purnell
| **Sampson MOONEY**
       bd. abt 1793, VA
       dd. bef 1859, Cherokee Co, AL
| & Delia (Dilla)
       bd. 1792, NC

Sampson Mooney served in the War of 1812, 3rd Regiment of the West Tennessee Militia Infantry, which fought in the Battle of New Orleans. He mustered in as a Private in November 1814 and was released from service in White County with the rank of 2d Sergeant in May 1815. Sampson and William's names appeared on numerous, separate White County deeds and court records for a couple of decades. They both received land grants from the State of Tennessee. As for Charles, he and Sampson both appeared on the 1826 tax list in the same area of White County TN. By the onset of the Civil War, all of the Mooney brothers from Virginia (that we know of) were dead, with the possible exception of William who was still living (age 75) in 1860 in Yalobusha County, Mississippi.

Sampson lived and owned land in Marion and Bledsoe Counties in Tennessee throughout the 1830's. By 1840 he was in Cherokee County, AL, farming on land purchased from the US Government Land Office. Land was plentiful and cheap and virtually everyone had some. Sampson paid $99.62 for 79 acres. By trade he was a blacksmith and gunsmith. The 1850 census was the first one to list the names of the families as well as the heads of household, so it was this census that provided the names of his wife, Delia (or Dilla or Delila), and four of their children. Almost nothing is known about Delia, not her maiden name nor the time and place of their marriage. Boaz was the oldest known child, born in 1813, probably in White County. While Sampson and his family were still in Cherokee County in 1850, Boaz was living in Bledsoe County TN. There may have been other children whose identities are unknown. Sampson died before 1859.

Sampson MOONEY
  bd. abt 1793, VA
  dd. bef 1859, Cherokee Co, AL
& Delia/Dilla
  bd. 1792, NC
| **Boaz "Bose" MOONEY**
| bd. 8 Jan 1813
| dd. 27 Feb 1865, Baileyton, Cullman Co, AL
| & Elizabeth
| bd. 13 May 1817, TN
| dd. 29 Oct 1888, AL
| **William M MOONEY**
| bd. abt 1821, TN
| & Mary
| bd. 1821, TN
| **Louisa MOONEY**
| bd. ca 1821, TN
| & Jonathan VARNER
| bd. 1813, GA
| **Charles MOONEY**
| bd. 1828
| **Mary MOONEY**
| bd. 1832, AL
| dd. AL
| & David BAIRD

```
|    bd. abt 1820, TN
|    dd. 4 Dec 1892, AL
| Marion MOONEY
|    bd. 1832
|    & Margaret
|    bd. 1845
| Isaac MOONEY
|    bd. 6 Jun 1834, TN
|    dd. 12 Jan 1912, Henryetta, Okmulgee, OK
|    & Lena/Seny Clementine DOWNS
|    bd. 6 Apr 1844, AL
|    dd. 15 Apr 1875, Briartown, Muskogee, OK
```

Boaz Mooney bought land in Cullman Co AL in 1858. This is where he and his wife Elizabeth and 6 of their children lived at the onset of the Civil War. Boaz was too old to fight, but his sons Franklin and George W. were to be pulled into the conflict. Like so many families in that terrible time, their loyalties were divided. Franklin was 21 when he enlisted in September of 1862 on the side of the Confederacy. There is no surviving record of his death. George W. enlisted for the Union in January of 1865, but died of typhoid fever before being mustered in. He was 19 when he died on May 1, 1865, a month after Lee surrendered at Appomattox. The third son Pierce was too young to fight. Boaz's sympathies were with the Confederacy but, ironically, he was murdered in 1865 by Confederate-sympathizing vigilantes, probably from the local home guard, who mistakenly believed he was hiding men avoiding service. The story of his murder tracked very closely to a story told by Boaz's grandson James Franklin and was verified in large part by an article in Morgan County's *Decatur Daily*, written July 12, 1964.

Boaz "Bose" MOONEY
bd. 8 Jan 1813
dd. 27 Feb 1865, Baileyton, Cullman Co, AL
& Elizabeth
bd. 13 May 1817, TN
dd. 29 Oct 1888, AL

```
|    Marian (Mary Ann, Polly) MOONEY
|       bd. 18 May 1838, TN
|       dd. Waldron, Scott Co, AR
|       & John Elijah WAGGONER
|       bd. 10 Aug 1837, AL
|       dd. 24 Jul 1911, Waldron, Scott Co, AR
```

| Franklin M. MOONEY
| bd. 29 Nov 1840, TN
| dd. 1863
| & **Elizabeth A. WIDENER**
| bd. 1839, GA
| dd. 1874
| **Isabella MOONEY**
| bd. 1842, AL
| & William KING
| **Jane Buncombe MOONEY***
| bd. 1844, AL
| & Unknown
| **Jane Buncombe MOONEY***
| bd. 1844, AL
| & A. H. DOTY
| **George W. MOONEY**
| bd. 1846, Bledsoe County, TN
| dd. 5 May 1865, Madison Station, AL
| **Martha MOONEY**
| bd. 1848, AL
| **Elizabeth MOONEY**
| bd. 1850
| & Sam C. CLARK
| bd. 1838
| **Pierce MOONEY**
| bd. 30 Sep 1852, Marshall Co, AL
| dd. 17 Sep 1895, Indian Territory, OK
| & Mary M. EVANS
| bd. Jun 1845, AL

There are few verifiable facts about Franklin. (We didn't even know his name until a few years ago when I connected with a descendant of Franklin's brother, Pierce Mooney.) Franklin's son James said that his father deserted to be with his wife, Elizabeth Widener, when their child was born, then returned to his unit and later died of disease. Probably Elizabeth and James went to live with her parents or other family after the war, but she's not listed with any of them in the 1870 census. In all likelihood, she was already remarried by 1870 and literally untraceable, since the husband's identity is not known.

Franklin MOONEY
bd. 29 Nov 1840, TN
dd. 1863
& **Elizabeth A. WIDENER**

bd. 1839, GA
dd. 1874
| **James Franklin Marion Jackson MOONEY**
| bd. 5 May 1863, KY or AL
| dd. 21 Feb 1940, Dell, AR

Prepared by Judy Underwood

35423256R00093

Made in the USA
Middletown, DE
02 October 2016